Sign up for our arts and culture newsletters at www.bronxarts.org

Cover image by Sofie Vasquez: *One Day in June. West Farms Square, The Bronx,* 2018

Edited by Crystal Valentine

Designed by Angel Hernandez and Priyanka Das

ISBN: 978-1070675626

ACKNOWLEDGMENTS

The Bronx Memoir Project launched with a series of free memoir writing workshops created by the Bronx Council on the Arts in spring of 2014, facilitated by a variety of BRIO award literary arts winners, as well as fiction writers, memoirists and poets from The Bronx.

The 2019 Bronx Memoir Project workshop series and Bronx Memoir Project – Volume III are made possible with funding from the New York City Department of Cultural Affairs in partnership with the City Council; New York State Council on the Arts with the support of Governor Andrew M. Cuomo and the New York State Legislature; Arts Midwest and the National Endowment for the Arts; and City Council members Andrew Cohen and Mark Gjonaj. Also supported in part by the Booth Ferris Foundation, Ovation, New Yankee Stadium Community Benefits Fund, Hispanic Federation, the City of New York, and the Department of Youth and Community Development.

Special recognition goes to Crystal Valentine for overseeing the 2019 workshop series, along with teaching artists Joseph Earl Thomas, Rich Villar, JD Debris, Peggy Robles-Alvarado, Caroline Rothstein, Porsha Olayiwola, Gbenga Adesina, and Jakki Kerubo. Also, Vanessa Mártir, Amy Gottlieb, and Orlando Ferrand for their leadership and guidance.

We also want to thank our workshop hosting organizations: the New York Public Library's Kingsbridge and Mott Haven branches, as well as the Poe Park Visitor Center and BronxArtSpace.

BRONX MEMOIR PROJECT

VOLUME III

Contents

COUNTING, WAITING

Diana Fu

It had been a long time since I took the subway from the Bronx to Queens.

I watched the trains and buildings change in a crowded cart; first, the decrepit buildings with their broken yellow windows like crooked teeth, empty lots teeming with such tall grass the chain link fence couldn't contain it. Then came the old historic brick buildings with steady white steam shooting out the chimneys before dispersing in the breeze. And lastly, the shining new apartments, with their cinnamon and beige smooth walls, lined with the aquamarine windows that never seemed to host any distinguishable curtain or flag like the others did. I watched the people changed too; their skin got lighter, bodies thinner. I watched them change from black, to brown, to white as we coursed through the city's underground.

We rumbled beneath the busy streets of Spanish Harlem, the Upper East Side, and Midtown East. I imagined all the thousands of feet and tires weighing down on us from above as the train stalled, again. I shut my eyes with intention, counting the seconds until the train would lurch forward again, shrinking away into the back of my seat.

At 42nd street, I dashed for my transfer. Past the belting musicians, insistent church pamphleteers, and overflowing newspaper stands, I made my way through the crowd like a salmon swimming upstream – desperate for one less minute amidst the stifling chaos of endless underground life. I slipped through the closing doors of a local train, recomposed myself, and found a seat at the end of a bench. Again, I shut my eyes and counted my breaths, the number of times I touched my tongue to my teeth.

When the light of day kissed my eyelids red, I opened my eyes to watch the silver skies and churches. Rooftop gardens. Korean and Chinese characters. When the doors opened at a station, I could smell the freshly wetted concrete – autumn rain in the city.

Suddenly, I wanted for my mother in a way I hadn't in years, not since I had left home for the first time. *When had she ceased to be the first person I wanted when the world became too much?* I thought of her on the other side of this mad continent, sleeping next to a cool open window, or perhaps lying awake under her covers, waiting for the sun to rise. *When had I grown old?*

I decided to text her about my special trip to Chinatown for the Mid-Autumn Festival mooncakes.

"妈妈！我今天去了皇后華埠！我买了月饼!"

I typed, glowing with quiet relief that I still remembered how to use pinyin, and that I still recognized the correct characters and grammar that my keyboard suggested. In my mind's eye, I imagined the slow grin spreading on my mother's face as she read my words: how happy she'd be that I still remembered the language she painstakingly taught me, even when my father insisted his children be raised as "Americans". How proud she would be of me now, as I was the only child left that still remembered the significance of the annual Mid-Autumn festival, and went out of my way to celebrate, even now as I lived alone in the Bronx.

I sent the text, and settled into the bench to watch more buildings go by. I counted the stops of the local 7 train. *Woodside. Sixty-ninth. Seventy-fourth and Broadway. Jackson Heights. Ninetieth Street, Elmhurst.*

I waited – no response. She was still asleep.

Over the years, I came to know my life in the city this way: counting and waiting. Counting and waiting for my subway stop. Counting the number of buses that passed me by, always waiting for the one that I needed. Counting my cash out for the week, sparingly, and waiting for the next paycheck. Counting the number of months, weeks, and days I had persevered away from home: too many and still not enough. And always, always waiting for the next opportunity to step onto a plane for my mother to fill my heart again.

TROUBLEMAKERS

Carol Foresta

Every day, after breakfast and before I go to sleep my Mama brushes my hair. I get 100 strokes. We count them together in quiet voices, practicing our English. Sometimes we get distracted and we talk about the old country where Bubbi used to brush my Mama's hair, which is long and straight although there is some silver mixed in with its dark brown almost black color. My Mama brushes her own hair before she works on mine. Sometimes we talk about how different my curly hair is and how much work it takes to get it straight enough to fit into the neat braids she knits together. It's a ritual. I love it and although she complains about how much time it takes and how it hurts her fingers to fight with my unruly locks, my Mama secretly loves it too. After all, my hair holds the secrets and the stories we tell each other.

Mama always smells good. Her clothes hold the fragrance of the meals she cooks. Her apron protects them from whatever splatters or spills from her baking. Her hands are strong but gentle, fingers flexible from years of braiding, sewing, knitting and kneading dough. Though she has so many talents, my mama is very excited and proud I am learning English and one day will speak in the language of our new country. She only speaks to me in Yiddish and English, refusing to speak in Polish because she says the Polish people murdered my grandparents, uncles, aunts and baby sister. It makes me sad to hear the stories of the trains and the long walks to the forest of Bronnaya Gora where the killing field still lives. Mama cries silently everyday when she talks of these things.

One day, there is no school and Mama decides we will walk to the barbershop together and bring my Papa his lunch. After carefully parting, brushing and braiding my hair she goes into the kitchen. I sit at the table and watch her cut up onions

13

and potatoes for the soup and sandwich she is preparing. I ask if I can help but Mama tells me I should just watch and learn. I know she is the best cook in the whole world so I watch everything and take pictures in my brain. I watch the shiny, sharp knife she uses to finely chop onions. I don't like the way the onions make my eyes feel. I wonder as she wipes away the tears running down her cheeks if they are drops of sadness or joy. Mama cries when she is both sad and happy.

Lunch is soon ready to bring to my Papa. Mama tucks her money into a cotton square, ties it in a knot and carefully places it in her brassiere nestled between her breasts where it will be safe. She will go to the store to buy food for dinner while I wait in the barbershop. I am excited to spend time there because people are always talking loud and fast in English and Yiddish while playing cards or getting shaves or haircuts. If there aren't any customers I climb up into the big chairs and move them around in a dizzying circle. I like the smell of the after shave lotion, and the sound of the voices accompanying the clicking of scissors and scraping of razors on skin.

When we reach the barbershop there is a crowd, the "boys" are there. They are customers and friends of my Papa. Some are salesmen, who carry large boxes tied with a rough twine and filled with shirts, others have cleaning supplies or newspapers to hawk. I like to see what they are schlepping. Some are waiting patiently for their turn so they can get back to business. Four large men in sports jackets are sitting at the folding table in the back of the shop playing pinochle and drinking schnaps. I can hear the cards slapping down on the tabletop, and the jingle of coins hitting the surface as bets are made, won or lost. It's warm here.

I watch my father as he slowly circles the chair in the center of the shop. He is a small trim man, not more than 5 feet tall. His hair is white and thin on top, and there are small puffs of it neatly patted down on the sides of his head. He wears a blue collared button down shirt tucked into brown slacks. Over the shirt he wears a white cotton uniform to protect his clothes from the lotions and creams he uses in his barbering. Mama waits patiently until Papa can take a break. I grab a broom and start sweeping up clumps of brown, black and grey hair that swirl like moths around the chairs. When Papa finishes expertly cutting the hair of his customer, he walks to the register. His shoulders are slumped and his steps are heavy. I hear the tapping of keys being pressed and the clang of the drawer popping open. He puts the money into the register and then heads over to Mama. He gratefully accepts the bag with food she has brought for his lunch.

I watch them talking quietly together, making plans. Papa gently touches Mama's hands and she looks into his eyes. The racket in the shop gets quieter when they are together. It's as if the room fills up with cotton. I want to hug them both but I continue sweeping. After all, my work is important. Mama puts on her coat on and tells me she will be back soon. I don't mind her leaving. There is so much action here I soon forget I am alone, the only child in this world of men.

After awhile, when no other customers are waiting for Papa to cut their hair or shave their faces he turns to me and tells me to hop up on the big dark brown leather chair. I put down my broom and feel rewarded. I nimbly climb the chair imagining it to be a throne. I inhale the sweet smell of shaving cream as it heats up close to where I perch. I see my reflection in the big mirror facing the chair. The whole shop is spread out behind and in front of me. For a few seconds I am the boss of it all. My Papa whispers secrets to me. We talk about how busy he is and how he will join the boys playing pinochle when all his work is done.

I rock in the barber chair from side to side, holding onto the stick with the ball on top. It makes the chair go up and down. I push the chair to the highest spot. I hoist myself even higher using my strong little arms. My sneakers slide and squeak on the slippery leather seat. I am proud of myself for being strong enough to lift myself. I swing my long chocolate braids from side to side. I feel powerful. I know the source of my strength is in my hair, lovingly cared for by my mama.

Papa's breath smells sweet. I watch him take his medicine. I see him lift the flask to his mouth before he comes over to my throne. With a big sweeping gesture he makes the white sheet billow out in front of us. It falls around my small body covering me from the neck down. It's fun to pretend to be a customer. I feel like I'm watching a magic show as I see him lift the gleaming silver scissors from the worktable and practice snapping them open and closed. They look like the mouth of a dangerous animal. I am glad it's Papa snipping them. I would not like to be near anyone else holding them in their hand. He tells me to sit still. I stop shifting from side to side, curious about what will happen next. I am surprised when my father's hairy hand pulls hard on my left braid. I never noticed how big his hand is, or how the veins stand out on it. I laugh nervously when he says, "You are one of the troublemakers, aren't you?" I think to myself, this is a new game. He's usually never arguing with my braid. I expect him to make a funny voice come out of it like he does with my doll. Instead, he snaps open his scissors and he hacks my hair off at the very top of its roots so close I can feel the steel blade cold against my scalp. My heart freezes but I do not utter a word of protest. My father then reaches around my small head and grasps its partner. This time he says, "And you are also responsible for so much hard work," as he snips and snaps it off.

My braids are both sitting in his hands and are no longer on my head. How will he put them back I wonder? Slowly I realize, as my father reaches for a brush and comb, this is not a magic show organized for my pleasure. Instead, it is my new reality. I hear my voice coming from deep in my chest as I scream my disapproval. I don't want him to touch me. I am afraid. I am angry. I squirm and writhe away from him like an injured animal. Papa is no longer to be trusted. I cover my head and body with the sheet like a shroud and crawl into a corner of the barbershop, planting myself underneath a stool with metal legs that barely offer protection. I sob and cry for a long time before I fall asleep. I wake when

I hear my mother saying, "Where are you Chavala? Why are you hiding?" I hear my father explaining quietly, "I just wanted to make things easier for you." My mother replying, "What do you mean?" My father, "You are always complaining about how much work it is to brush her hair." My mother, "Nu, it's a job but I don't mind, what happened?" My father, "I didn't think she'd get so mad, I only cut her hair, she didn't let me finish." My mother, "What did you do? Without talking with me? I am the Mama! Who asked you to interfere? How could you do such a thing? Go away. Have you no *rakhmones*?" she suffers. "*Oy vey* es mere. Chavala, let me see you." She tugs at the sheet and pulls me carefully out from under my safe place. She tries in vain to put the fragments of trust back together. The ritual is broken. The stories are finished. The troublemakers executed.

REWIND, FAST FORWARD, LEAPS OF FAITH

Yvette Gonzalez

Rewind. I went out the door first; Mami was still inside. I ran down the hall corridor in my short dress and patent leather shoes and stopped at the top of the stairs. I crouched my body halfway and looked down at the long set of marble stairs, carefully calculating the distance between the top stair and the landing below. It seemed like a long way down but I had to figure out how I would do this, how I would make this jump. My arms were slightly bent and my hands gripped my knees as I stared down and focused on that landing below. Without further hesitation, I lunged forward and leaped into the air, my small body soaring weightlessly, hands still gripping my knees, and landed in crouched position inches away from the bottom stair and onto the landing. I remained there for a few minutes, unafraid and pleased with my daring feat. I was neither shaken nor scared, until I heard Mami's voice above. "¡Mira muchacha, te vas a matar!" - "Little girl, you're going to kill yourself!" Mami rushed down the stairs and grabbed my hand and we walked out the building door. I was two years old when I took that first leap of faith.

At four years old I took another leap of faith. Mami took me to the park and lifted me up onto the metal swing, pushing the seat bar up and lowering it securely down so I wouldn't fall out. She gave the swing the first push and walked away. I continued to swing on my own, higher and higher, looking up at the blue sky and looking down at the rough concrete below. I spotted a sparrow flying directly in front of me. In an instant I zeroed in and calculated the sparrow's movement. I quickly lifted the metal bar and leaped out of the swing and into the air with my arms extended in front of me, hands and fingers spread out like a fan. I caught the sparrow in mid-flight, cupping my hands and gently clutching its little body. I landed on the cement floor below in crouched position, pleased with my accomplishment and slightly smiling. I gazed down at the sparrow with its soft brown feathers and then set it free. Mami rushed over and exclaimed "Te vas a matar, muchacha!"— "You're going to kill yourself, little girl!"

I was still four years old when my family decided to go on a Sunday trip to the Statue of Liberty. I had on a lovely little Spring coat; knees exposed under the flare of its hem. It was a beautiful warm day and there were many people walking around. My family was waiting online outside the Statue. I wandered off but remained directly in eye's view of them. I walked over to a grassy area and looked down upon it and then up at the blue sky when I spotted a sparrow in flight. I followed it with my eyes, never losing focus, as it landed a few feet away from me on the grass. I stared it down & quickly calculated the distance between myself & the sparrow. I leaped forward and upwards, arms extended, hands fanned out. Like a large sparrow in flight, I landed within an inch of it, my Spring coat flaring and body sliding with little legs spread out. I scooped up the sparrow gently and looked at it, once again, pleased with my feat. I then remembered that Mami would soon be coming for me, so I got up and set the sparrow free. I brushed myself off, with not one scratch on me, and wandered back to my family. Mami glanced at me but hadn't noticed what I had done.

Fast Forward. I went out the door first; my life's partner was still inside, or had he gone out first? I looked down at the long set of wooden stairs, carefully calculating each step I would take in my descent towards the landing below. I had on comfortable clothing and sneakers which helped me to focus on the long task ahead of me. I was a little scared but remained calm and quiet. I was taking a big risk, but it was for the good of my health, so I was pleased with my decision. Many, many hours went by and I woke up in my hospital bed wanting to be in crouched position, with arms straight and close to both sides of my body and hands slightly spread. I thought of all the leaps I had taken; of the little sparrows I had caught. I now felt like a captured sparrow, unable to move and wanting to be set free. As the days passed and I slowly and painfully recovered, I was finally set free. However, I knew that I would never recover properly if I did not take yet another leap of faith. For a long time things had not been good between my partner and I, so after more than 30 years I leaped forward, suspended in midair, clutching myself and landing on my own two feet. How I wish Mami was there, rushing to my side, to grab my hand and walk me out of this. I wanted to hear her words, "Muchacha, no te preocupes, de esto no vas a morir!"— "Little girl, don't worry, you won't die from this!" I was all grown up now and wondered what other leaps of faith I would take.

HAIR TODAY....GONE TOMORROW

Pauline Graham Binder

I've always liked my hair. It was thick and strong, healthy African hair. It wasn't long and wavy down my back like my sister Birdy's or as long as my late mother's. But when Aunt Daphne would comb my hair and put one ribbon in the front and two in the back of my shoulder-length hair I could not have been prouder.

I can see myself going to infant school in my white blouse and blue jumper, carrying my slate and chalk in a bag. Then sitting on a long bench at the school with other children singing "Hey diddle diddle, the cat and the fiddle. The cow jumped over the moon," my two back braids hitting my shoulder as I moved my head from side to side while chanting and clapping. The one period when I didn't like my hair was when I went to live with Aunt Clare in Kingston. She would comb my hair roughly and when I cried out, she'd hit me in the head with the comb. That's when I wished I had hair that was easier for the comb to go through. But back then they didn't believe in running a hot comb through a young girl's hair to straighten it. My hair was first straightened when I was fifteen. It was the day before my brother Gilly and I left Port Antonio, the beautiful seaside town where we had been living with our father until he abandoned us to go live with a woman. We were returning to Clarendon to live with Aunt Daphne and where my God-sent benefactor, Mr. Nash, could help me. My hair straightening was done by a lady named Miss Scott, one of the many neighbors who gave us food and encouragement during that terrible time. Her legs were bent and she was unable to walk. She was a dressmaker who couldn't pedal her Singer sewing machine. Her relatives and friends would work the pedal by hand. Both Gilly and I became part of her pedal brigade which helped her to earn a living by making beautiful clothes. The other thing she did was hair. I remember being quite skittish when she put the hot comb and curling iron on the coal stove. I worried about being burnt by those implements. But she assured me that there was nothing to worry about, but I had to sit still. No moving while she worked on my hair. After she was done, I loved what I could see. My hair was longer and bouncy, and I felt sophisticated like the women in the district who worked in offices and wore tight hobble skirts and red Cutex on their fingernails.

When I arrived in the Bronx in 1964, age sixteen, all the Black women with whom I came in contact wore straightened hair achieved by hot comb or chemicals. It was frowned upon if you didn't straighten your hair. But by 1969 when I was returning to Jamaica, the natural Afro hair movement in America was in full swing. My last act of defiance before leaving Aunt Clare's apartment to go back to Jamaica on July 1, 1969, was to refuse to go to the hairdresser to get my hair done. I must admit that act was simply to irritate her for all the hell she had put me through. She wore a hairstyle that looked like Ella Fitzgerald's and the women of that era. I could hear my aunt on the phone complaining to her friends that I was going back to Jamaica without getting my hair done. She did not like the natural hairstyle and complained about women wearing Afros.

Of course, shortly after arriving in Jamaica I went and got my hair straightened. It was in a very healthy state, thick and bouncy. Once when I was walking down the road, this guy I was seeing was driving by and said he recognized me from the back by my hair. By 1970 I was back in NY still straightening my hair, but by 1971 I started wearing a natural hairstyle. At first it was just my own hair which I braided myself, no enhancements. Then by 1972 I was sporting a righteous Afro and did for many years. It must have been in the 1980s that I went back to straightening my hair. In the 1990s people told me I had Oprah hair. I was very proud especially when some said I actually looked like Oprah. It was 1998, when I first had my hair professionally braided with attachments. Then people started telling me I looked like Whoopi Goldberg. Once, my son Andrew and I were standing outside a store in Yonkers waiting for my husband when a woman thought I was actually Whoopi Goldberg! Up to 2016, when I took out the braids and combed out my hair, I said Dante Deblasio, the mayor's son, had nothing on me. My hair stood up in all its glory, a righteous Afro again. But I didn't wear it that way anymore. I went back to straightening it. By then my hair had really grown and at my 2016 birthday get together with friends I was complimented at how good my hair looked. And I had to agree. Then sometime in 2017 I was horrified every time I combed my hair and it was coming out by the handful! Moroccan Argan oil, and Jamaican black castor oil were recommended. They didn't help. Things only got worse. I went to see a dermatologist and she prescribed and sold me shampoo, conditioner, and pills and they may have worked somewhat. But she wanted to get my doctor's permission to give me cortisone shots in my head. Not being up for that, I never went back.

I was never keen on the very short haircuts some women were sporting because I didn't think it would fit my face. But sometime in 2018 I went to the hairdresser and got my hair cut down to the nub! Surprisingly, I've gotten many compliments and have found the lack of hair quite freeing. No rollers. No sitting for hours on end getting braids put in. I'm getting used to the look. And I have come to the conclusion that I shouldn't worry about hair so much. Instead be grateful that at age 70 I'm still above ground, hair or no hair!

MY ALMOST DATE

Jacqueline Reason

I think I went on a date Saturday night, but I'm still not sure. Maybe he is bipolar, on the lamb, or as my friend suggested, a serial killer. My almost date occurred at the spring flower show at the Bronx Botanical Gardens. My Aunt Suzy questioned why I didn't have my new friend pick me up. She had already commented on my deep analysis for what was only, possibly, a first date. First dates, according to my aunt, were grand opportunities and always the lady's choice.

I barely made it to the lobby, when Richard called and asked if I was at the venue yet.

"I'm getting in the cab now." I answered.

I planned to arrive early but didn't anticipate there would be a deluge of April showers. A half hour later, Richie greeted me with a soft hug and sweet kiss on the cheek. After taking one look at my dainty floral umbrella, Richie debonairly pulled out a large, golf umbrella. When the wind destroyed it in five seconds, he calmly suggested that we stop at the bookstore to wait out the torrential winds.

I lost sight of Richie for a few minutes, as the gift shop was teeming with people. He reappeared saying he had "coincidentally" run into an old friend who happened to be at the show as well.

"Can she join us?" Richie asked.

I was skeptical, dumbfounded, and disappointed. What should I have said? I mumbled "No," but audibly uttered, "Sure, whatever you'd like."

After all, I wasn't sure this was even a date. While I waited for Richie to return, every scenario I could think of played in my mind. This was all a rouse to make her, whoever she was, jealous. She's going to be young, thin and fucking gorgeous and I was going to absolutely lose it. In the middle of my millionth thought, the two returned arm in arm.

"Let me introduce you to my friend, Jackie." Richie said as she looked right past me. After Richie nudged her, she responded, "Duh".

Even though I was thinking, "What the fuck does duh mean?" I shook her hand with all the confidence in the world. Besides, I needed to project my best game face to keep myself from shedding the single tear welling up in the corner of my right eye.

The friend is an attractive woman. Her hairstyle is slightly Jerseylicious and her Covergirl eyelashes reflected a spider-like eeriness. Like mine, the edges of her body were soft. As we stood in line for the event, I caught a side profile in the full-length mirrors along the wall. I was pleasantly surprised at how good I looked and even more pleased to declare "better ass" definitely went to me.

The conservatory was impressive; however, we were all equally disappointed that the anticipated live band was replaced by a deejay and Mac computer. The venue, lit primarily by flickering candlelight, appeared stylish and romantic. When I told my aunt about Richie's choices, she was genuinely impressed. He'd asked about Wave Hill and some museum tours of famous dwellings downtown. There was even a suggestion about Jake's, "the best steakhouse in the Bronx," overlooking Van Cortland Park.

"He sounds like a man of sophisticated taste." That was a rave for Auntie.

Our phone calls never made it to an intimate level. I made sure my answers were short and to the point; so I didn't provide too much miscellaneous information about a failed twenty year marriage, returning to New York, etcetera, etcetera.

"Listen for ice cubes. Pay attention to the patterns concerning the time of day for phone calls. Could there be a wife or girlfriend? Is he calling while she's at work, or in the shower?" These, according to my aunt, were all tell-tale signs of trifling men.

Richie was shorter than I realized, about five eight or so. He wore kind of a J Crew special, tucking his shirt into the belt around his slender waist. I wasn't surprised by Richie's attention to detail. It was his tailored suit and coordinating ties that made him stand out when he came into the Bronx Library Center.

I was a volunteer at the employment center on the fifth floor that was always filled with crowds of people. Most were working class folk. But on occasion, an unemployed professional come in seeking a fresh spin on a resume. Theoretically, Richie and I were at an advantage, educated professionals with years of steady work history. However, advantageous was far from what we were feeling.

As Richie and I walked shoulder to shoulder through the crowds, I took pictures of the gorgeous, fragrant flowers and engaged in effortless conversation. We routinely waited for the young woman to catch up with us. She mentioned she was a pastry chef and wanted pictures of the flowers so she could recreate them with sugar paste. I was confused when no one spoke of spouses, children, or past relationships. Instead the talk was of career paths, the economy and layoffs. Maybe, I didn't quite get what the modern life was supposed to be. Would this be my new normal?

On completing our first loop of the observatory, our companion bought us all our second round of drinks. "Gin and tonic with a twist of lime" she said. I forget what Richie drank, but I ordered red wine. I regretted my order immediately. I hate tepid, alcohol. I didn't stress outwardly. I just sipped with grace, making certain to maintain my composure and judgment in this peculiar situation.

"To a wonderful night." Richie toasted.

"Cheers" I chimed in, all three of us clicking our plastic barware.

Against the backdrop of music, dim lights and whirlwind movement, we began to loosen up, enjoy the crowd and the ambience of the evening. A couple of times, Richie took my hand so we didn't get separated and later I held on to his upper arm to keep up with him. To my surprise there were solid muscles under his small frame and I didn't feel him tense from my touch.

Richie stopped to point out the flowers and tell me the scientific names of the hanging ferns and other plant species. I started to wonder if he was testing my interest in the plants, so I asked him if he was trying to impress me. Richie replied yes and asked if it was working.

The friend interrupted with, "I already knew those names."

"What was your name again?" I questioned.

I really had forgotten. But I have to admit. I was pleased by her frustration and subsequent silence. As we continued walking through the quixotic setting of waterfalls and candlelight, I asked Richie if he was a gardener. He laughed and said every year he attempted, never quite successfully, to maintain a small one at his house near Orchard Beach.

"Perhaps you can help me become better at many things over the summer." Richie suggested.

Somewhere among the chatter and the drinks, the alcohol began to take its effect and I heard Richie say he was near suicidal when we met. I didn't respond verbally, but I thought about those days among the chaos in the library. Perhaps he and I felt trapped in some alternate universe and that was our attraction to each other.

When it was obvious that Richie and I were exchanging some intimate moments, suddenly, the former co-worker commented on how beautiful I was. I thanked her for the compliment without returning it. What if they were both bisexual and this was some freaky, friendship experiment? Slowly, our dinner companion started unravelling in front of us. She walked up to men standing alone and asked them if they thought I was beautiful.

"We're going to find you a boyfriend." She said as she began stealing the flameless candles in their frosted holders and stuffing them into the deep pockets of her black trench coat. She started taking selfies with total strangers, followed by photo bombing groups and dropping candles into the purses of unsuspecting women.

"Would you like a candle?" She asked me as her pockets began to glow.

"I'll buy you candles." Richie begged her to put them back.

Embarrassed, Richie pulled me to the side and whispered "I'm so sorry. The next time won't be like this."

Richie continued consuming glasses of the complimentary bourbon cocktail and extended our getting to know you conversation. I began to get tipsy, but nowhere near the spectacle of my female counterpart. Richie and I agreed it was time for dinner and some bread for our inebriated chum. We decided to eat on Arthur Avenue, the Bronx's Little Italy. Our companion exclaimed that she was Italian, thereby establishing her expertise on the cuisine and everything else.

Richie braved the coat check line, leaving the co-worker and me to exchange pleasantries. She told me about her life, her hobbies and her childhood; but when some statement in her conversation indicated she learned about me before tonight Richie arrived just in time to cut her off.

Finally, comfortable in my midnight skin, I realized I had nothing to prove to anyone. Even without being a Cornell graduate, or Wall Street trader, I held my own in a conversation without telling a story about being a mom or grandmother. I informed Richie I was calling it a night, gave him a peck on the cheek and thanked him and our dinner companion, who had now composed herself, for a lovely evening and took my little umbrella out to the waiting cabstand down the cobblestone street.

MOM AND HER TWO ANNS

Gloria S. Lanzone

"Auntie Ann, did you know that Mom wanted a Raggedy Ann doll very badly when she was a little girl? But you were all so poor, she was afraid to ask for one," I said. It was a hot summer afternoon in the Bronx in the mid-1960s. I was relaxing with a glass of iced tea and Auntie Ann was sitting in our kitchen reading the newspaper.

I wore my favorite red tank top and blue shorts and my dangling legs were draped over the arm of the blue living room chair. I was a sophisticated young teen letting her adored aunt in on a closely guarded family secret.

Auntie Ann was Mom's eldest sister, ten years her senior, dynamic and outspoken, yet warm, gregarious, caring and fiercely protective of her loved ones, most notably her baby sister. "Your grandfather said the wheels in her brain were always turning," Mom said to me years later.

Some considered her too authoritarian, but I loved her and was her constant companion. Our favorite activity was shopping at Klein's, Korvettes, or Alexander's on Fordham Road. She parked in a garage close to Jerome Avenue and we walked hand in hand to Alexander's. My mom didn't drive, so travelling by car instead of the bus was a special treat.

As the words sank in, Auntie Ann raised her eyebrows, crossed her arms and stood stiff as the living room wall. "What!" she exclaimed. "I never knew that!" She paced the living room while running a hand through her wavy thick short gray hair. I recognized her go-getter attitude as she smirked ever so slightly with narrowed eyes. I awaited the outcome of her outburst with a similar smirk and jiggling feet.

"Oh yes," I said. "She told me yesterday after she took the chicken out of the oven. I told her I wanted a toy oven when I was a little kid. My friend Ginny had one and I wanted one just like it. You know, Auntie Ann, she looked so sad. She said she was so sorry and that she understood what it felt like to want something so badly. That's when she told me about Raggedy Ann."

"Well, well," Auntie Ann said pointing her right index finger at me. "You do know where we're going tomorrow, don't you?"

"No," I said, staring back at her, my big brown eyes wide in questioning anticipation. "Where?" I asked in a loud whisper.

"To Gimbels to buy her one, that's where," she shouted. And, that's just what we did. The next morning, off to Cross County in Yonkers we went.

My mother never told anyone except me that she secretly longed for a Raggedy Ann doll. She was a shy youngster growing up on Summit Avenue in the Highbridge section of the Bronx during the Great Depression in the 1930s, the youngest of four girls in a poor household that included her parents, aunt and uncle. She was used to hand-me-downs, and never asked for anything because they couldn't afford much. So, she never told anyone of her heart's desire. If there was food on the table, they were happy and would survive.

During the Great Depression, the only toys, if a family could afford them, were bicycles, wagons, dolls or roller skates. My grandparents could afford only one gift for each of their girls. "Children considered themselves lucky to get this one toy," Mom said. "We never felt deprived because everyone was in the same boat. Besides, so much love and family tradition warmed our hearts ... Christmas trees, men exchanging homemade bottles of wine, and making homemade cookies courtesy of Marietta."

Marietta was the master baker from my grandfather's hometown of Barletta, near Bari, Italy. Each year, early in the morning, she arrived at the home of her extended family in the Bronx. Her self-assumed right was making an abundant supply of cookies for the family to enjoy or give as gifts. She made the rules, however, so the women and children could only watch and learn, not contribute to this baking ritual, except via such

30

mundane tasks as greasing cookie sheets. "Simple things made us so happy," Mom reminisced. "So different from the way life is today."

In the early 1930s, Mom was in the second or third grade in Public School 73, when the teacher brought her own Raggedy Ann to class, put the doll on the desk and read a Raggedy Ann story to the children. "I loved her little white pinafore and bright eyes. She looked like she'd be a good friend," Mom said. "I identified with her because life was so simple and so was she. It was love at first sight."

Mom was in her early 40s on that hot August afternoon long ago when I presented her with the rectangular box wrapped in her favorite color blue wrapping paper. "It's from me and Auntie Ann," I said with a smile worthy of a toothpaste commercial. "Hurry up … open it," I said, jumping up and down.

Auntie Ann's brown eyes glistened with silent satisfaction as Mom tore at the wrappings. She stared at the beloved doll, tears flowing down her face as she hugged Raggedy Ann, box and all. Memories of hard times and a childhood yearning came flooding back like a gentle golden tide at sunset. She then reached out, took Auntie Ann's hand and hugged and kissed it too.

"I told Auntie Ann you always wanted Raggedy, so she bought it for you," I said. "Isn't that great?"

"Great? Oh yes. Great. I love you both so much," Mom said in her teary, squeaky voice.

My aunt's love for my mom was so powerful, it transcended the Great Depression and poverty. She fulfilled her little sister's silent wish 30 years later. I loved Auntie Ann even more that I did before. She came through for mom, and at the same time, taught her young niece, me, her first lesson in love.

For the first time, I saw the process of love unfold firsthand. Not parental love, but a powerful emotion bonding family through both hard and rewarding times.

Auntie Ann's sensitive and tender gesture laid a compassionate foundation for my life. Her instinctive loving mind-set became my own. If someone needs empathy, I do what comes naturally ... reach out with support.

As for myself, if I need an emotional or inspirational boost, I go into mom's bedroom and hug Raggedy Ann close to my heart.

LESSON FOR A FOREIGNER

Cheryl McCourtie

The car pulled onto the shoulder of the road and came to an abrupt halt. My mother's arm shot out in front of me to keep me from becoming a projectile. Ram Chandra, at the wheel, squinted behind his wire-rim glasses and watched silently until the speeding cars that had now overtaken us disappeared around the next bend. None of us were wearing a seatbelt.

My family and I were returning to Liberia's capital, Monrovia, after a summer vacation in August of 1969. We had visited my parents' native island of Jamaica, and my mother's mother, Grandma Bethune, and her sister, Aunt Cynthia, in New York. Through my seven-year-old eyes, New York was a dirty city with lots of concrete, big mismatched buildings, and people who scurried about like hamsters with mean faces. Our relatives there worked all the time, talked about "the job" as if it were a serving of Brussels sprouts and never seemed to have fun like we did in Liberia. I was glad to be going home. And home then to me was Liberia, where we had been living since I was three. Where we had been living since I had memory.

On the eight-hour straight flight from New York to Monrovia, I polished off my meal of Cornish stuffed hen (the menu on this route for more than a decade) and colored carefully and deliberately in my Pan Am coloring book. My kids kit included a brooch, and I carefully packed it away in my blue and white plastic Pan Am carry-on bag. I would wear it to school on my first day in my new second grade class, when we would talk about what we did for the summer. Mommy told me it was time to sleep and turned off the overhead light. I nodded off, using her arm as my pillow until landing time.

In Monrovia Daddy's friend and colleague on his UN agricultural team, Ram Chandra, surprised us at the airport. As we exited customs, we saw him waving to us, a broad smile animating his pleasant features. We piled into his apple-red car with a summer worth of matching green Samsonite luggage, bubbling over with news from the other side of the world. Daddy took the front seat with Ram Chandra, and the two friends slipped into comfortable banter about adult things, like politics and work. Bo-ring.

The two-lane highway was slick with rain. It was the rainy season, which lasts from May to October. It rained every day, then, and the skies split in two as thunder punctuated white hot lightning. The vegetation that sprung up on either side of the highway was green and lush in the darkness, the ferns waving with the wind, as if in greeting.

Then we saw persistent lights behind us on the unlit road. Two cars were racing with each other at breakneck speed. It is then that Ram Chandra pulled over. The cars whizzed past us and the wind tunnel they created rocked our vehicle. "Ridiculous," Ram Chandra muttered.

"Their houses must be on fire," Daddy said, chuckling good naturedly. Not long afterward we heard skidding and an ear-splitting bang—the sound of metal on metal. When we approached the bend, we saw that the two cars had crashed. We slowed down, and then stopped. A man appeared seemingly out of nowhere, staggering toward the car, his arms extended, his clothes shredded like the fringe outfits that were all the rage. He was wide-eyed and covered with blood.

He collapsed against the car. Red blood on the red car. "Help me, help me," he croaked. He looked like a crazy monster in the scary movies that I couldn't watch through to their inevitable, gory conclusions. I was shaking, and the moment I reached out for my mother, she had already reached out for me. She grabbed me and shielded my face in her stomach. I couldn't breathe.

We were foreigners who had narrowly missed being in an accident with Liberians. While Liberia is a country that was founded on myriad migrations—from Africa and the Americas—its nationals regarded outsiders with a healthy dose of suspicion. Foreigners, particularly white foreigners (which we were not) who raised the ire of Liberians with racially prejudiced peccadillos, were packed up and deported overnight. What were we to do? Fear spread like a scotch bonnet pepper swallowed whole. The adults conferred in urgent, whispered tones. I heard the names ELWA and JFK, two major hospitals, and the words die and incident.

And then I slipped into my fantasy world: At Ram Chandra's urging my mother and I scampered into the third-row collapsible seats of his Peugeot 504. Daddy and Ram Chandra gingerly helped the injured man into the first row of passenger seats and leaned him against the door. They bolted to the mangled cars, and after some huffing and puffing and an exchange I couldn't make out, they lifted an unconscious man and woman from the wreckage. They placed the two floppy rag-doll figures on the seat in Ram Chandra's car beside the first man, who had begun to make gurgling sounds. "Mommy, Mommy." I was crying hysterically now, my voice muffled by my mother's dress. I was inconsolable.

"Shhhh. Be quiet." Because of our heroics, the Liberians lived to race again.

No such heroics took place. In reality we drove off to get help, leaving the accident survivors at the scene. From my calculations now, we most likely went to the ELWA hospital in Paynesville, which is much closer to the airport than JFK in downtown Monrovia. Ram Chandra was driving his own vehicle, probably a six-seater American car, not a 9-seater Peugeot, UN's vehicle of preference, which would have been white or UN baby blue, not red. All of us couldn't have travelled in the compact car. Ram Chandra would have had to leave some of us on the road in the dark and rain to make room for the injured. Who in my family would we have chosen to stand as sentries in the storm?

Being Good Samaritans would not have worked in this situation. If we had taken the accident survivors in our car, a

35

car driven by a foreigner and occupied by other foreigners, and they died on the way to the hospital, it could have set off a diplomatic maelstrom.

When I asked my parents about this event decades later, they exchanged hooded looks, and expressed surprise about the depths of my memory. They assured me that the drag racers did survive the trauma.

The memory of this event was buried for years, until recently, when an elderly woman was run over on 263rd Street and Riverdale Avenue in the Bronx, around the corner from my building. The deceased was the victim of a youthful driver who was drag racing, just as those drivers were on those slick roads from the airport in Liberia so many years ago. A lifetime ago.

There was a bloody coup in Liberia in 1980, and a decade later it plunged into a civil war that lasted for 14 years. The country that I considered as home on that Pan Am flight disappeared into the madness, and the friends that I had made dispersed across the world, immigrating to new, strange countries as my family and I did, or returning to their native countries. Ram Chandra repatriated to India. My mother died. Even Pan Am met its demise.

I am now one of those people who—overscheduled and multitasked beyond reasonableness— scurries. For many years I worked on the "the job," which I refused to discuss with family and friends during my time off, my revolt against Brussels sprouts. My revolt against the bitter taste meaningless work left in my mouth. Liberia hasn't been my home for decades. Jamaica, where my parents are from, has never been my home. Here in America I am considered a foreigner, too. A Black foreigner. Especially now.

Home is somewhere. I don't know where, just yet. Maybe someday I will.

MELROSE AVENUE - WELCOME THE STRANGER

André P.

"I'm looking for a place to stay. I don't have much money", I wrote in an email. This was something like a small Catholic monastery in the Bronx.

"We don't do intake by email," said the reply. "Call us."

I called them. "I'm looking for a place to stay. I don't have much money. Can I come?" "Sure." "When is the best time?" "Before 5 o'clock." "Who should I ask for?" "Brother Frank."

I got on the #5 train uptown. The ride took about half an hour. I got off at Third Avenue and 149th Street, the third station in the Bronx. This was a six-way intersection, with 149th Street going east-west, Melrose Ave. to the north becoming Willis Ave. to the south, and Third Avenue crossing them at a 30-degree angle. The intersection and the area is known as "the Hub", because of bustling human traffic converging on the busy shopping area—clothing, furniture, electronics

—and because several elevated train lines had crossed or terminated there.

I walked up Melrose Avenue.

Melrose Avenue was filled with greasy-spoon restaurants, delis, bodegas, a few cell phone stores, a tax preparer office, and a surprising number of hair salons and barbershops. There was a firehouse; a police station that served the numerous housing projects nearby, one of which the source of a Legionnaires' disease epidemic that summer; and a laundromat. I turned the corner. I passed a somewhat run-down old tenement house, with a sign proclaiming it a site of a "project" named after a multi-eyed dog from Greek mythology. The next house was cleaner and in better shape. I pressed the buzzer.

"Yes?" a male voice answered from the intercom. "I'm André, I called." "Come in." The door buzzed, I pulled it open, walked into a small vestibule, with another glass door, a narrow hallway behind it, and a window in the wall to my right.

"Hi, I'm John, I'm a volunteer," said a young man from behind the desk inside. "Come in." I entered the hallway and stood in the door to his office. "So, you want to stay with us?"

"Yes." "Would you be able to pass a drug test?" "Yes." (We already went through that over the phone.) "We do breathalyzer tests every evening, and random drug tests; would you be OK with that?" "Yes." "Now, I'd like you to give me all your clothes, I'll wash them and give them back to you. This is to keep bedbugs away. I'll give you something to wear." He led me to a small room next to the office, gave me a large black plastic bag, a pair of sweatpants, a V-neck T-shirt, and disappeared, closing the door. I changed and put all my clothes in the bag. I had the clothes I was wearing, and another change, like Mother Teresa and her nuns.

"Ready", I told John from outside the office and handed him the bag with my clothes. "Now take your things, I'll show you to your room," he said and put the bag on the floor. We went deeper into the hallway. There was a door on the left, then the hallway widened to an elevator, next to which was a set of stairs. We took the elevator to the fifth floor. Upstairs, there was a larger hallway, a door to another lounge-like space with a sofa, a large clock above it, a cross, a statue, some chairs, and printed reproductions of religious paintings on the walls. One hallway opened ahead of us, leading to a window in the wall opposite the street, another went back behind a wall towards the street. We went forward. There were several rooms and two bathrooms. All the rooms except the first on the left had no doors. We stopped in front of the last room on the right. "This is your room," said John.

The room was small but not too small, had a window overlooking the back yard and the two- floor houses on the next street, a wooden captain's bed with drawers, a three-drawer dresser, a chair, a closet, and a cross on the wall. On the dresser was a copy of the Bible and the Catechism of the Catholic Church, 2nd edition. "Neat," I thought.

"I'll leave you here", said John. "Dinner's at 7 in the dining room, but come sometime before that, we'll do the intake." "Sure. Thanks."

I put down my things and picked up the Catechism. The Bible is the word of God, it's deep, beautiful, written in a simple language, but hard to understand if one is looking for a set of directions. By contrast, the Catechism lays out the Catholic Christian doctrine in contemporary language, bit after bit after bit, organized into parts, chapters, sections, and numbered paragraphs, with almost every statement linked to a supporting reference in the Bible, papal encyclicals, and theologians' treatises. It reads like a user's manual to life as a Christian, written by a German theology professor or a Boeing engineer who was given enough time. I opened the Catechism on a random page and saw paragraph 2241. "The more prosperous nations are obliged, to the extent they are able, to welcome the foreigner in search of the security and the means of livelihood which he cannot find in his country of origin. Public authorities should see to it that the natural right is respected that places a guest under the protection of those who receive him." I found out later that pretty much everyone was from another state or country. The handful of native Bronxites were friendly and welcoming to the rest of us. Dinner time was approaching. I went to the dining room downstairs. Three rows of tables, crosses, reproductions of religious paintings, a three-dimensional reproduction of da Vinci's "The Last Supper", one photo of a smiling 60+ man in a brown habit (the founder of this small religious order), a Bible on a stand, wall clock, whiteboard. Residents were filing in, taking seats, talking leisurely. This was not a City-funded pressure cooker. At 7 sharp, a Brother came to the front of the room, led us in reciting "Our Father", and read a passage from the Bible in English and in Spanish, the two official languages of the Bronx.

Then we formed a line to the kitchen window, picked up plates of food, returned to our seats, and ate. Real food, the way God made it, cooked from basic ingredients, with care. No chemicals.

After dinner, some of us went upstairs, some stayed to play board games. A novice from a friary in Harlem played a volunteer. The novice seemed to be self-taught, didn't follow a large library of memorized openings, but improvised unorthodox and unusual moves, hard to predict or defeat. He was more like a great jazz player than a classical musician. I liked his style. Shower in one of the two private bathrooms (other floors had three, but 12 residents each, ours only 6), lights out at 10pm. At 5:30 the next morning, a Brother came from room to room, knocking gently on the wall to wake us up.

In the morning, we all had assigned work. My job was to sweep and mop the hallway on my floor. I was told that the duties rotated every month. Some residents cleaned other hallways, some bathrooms, some the recreation room on the second floor, some washed up after breakfast, some after dinner. There was no lunch; we were allowed to make bagels with cream cheese and take them with us. We ended the breakfast with a prayer, and had to be out by 7 am, 7 days a Week. We had group activities in the evening: games on Fridays, which sharpened our minds; free nights or movie nights on Saturdays and Sundays (preselected DVDs played on a large flat-screen TV in the recreation room), and, rarely, baseball or football on TV; house meetings on Mondays; unloading a truck of donated food brought by a grocer called "uncle Barney" on Tuesdays, always after an announcement that this is entirely voluntary; Bible study with clerics invited from the Yonkers seminary on Wednesdays and Thursdays. There were services on Sundays in the beautifully restored church on the same compound. We were not required to attend, but more than half of us did. Thirty residents of various ages, about a dozen Fathers, Brothers, volunteers, and novices, all pretty well integrated, no disharmony.

After about a week of this quasi-monastic routine, a thought came to me out of the blue, and surprised me by its double-edged nature: "They appear genuine."

DIVINE AWAKENING

Stan Greenberg

I really wanted to spend the evening of April 25, 2017 at the 42nd Street Library. Two of my favorite authors, Mary Karr and Elif Batuman, would be speaking. However, the tickets were sold out within hours of going on sale.

Instead, I (along with my wife, Nina) attended the symposium sponsored by Manhattan College - located not far from the Van Cortlandt stop of the #1 train.

Once there, we met Marianne. She later told us that she attends an Episcopal Church located in the Kingsbridge area of the Bronx. She suggested that we attend coffee hour which takes place on the last Sunday of every month.

It wouldn't be until late July that Nina and I visited the church for the first time. We attended the 10:00 mass. The priest blessed us. Downstairs, Marianne introduced us to the priest-in-charge whom I learned was named Mother Loyda, a kind and beneficent woman. She is Puerto Rican and told us that contrary to popular assumption not all Hispanics are Roman Catholic.

Notwithstanding the shakiness of my faith in God at the time, we visited the Church on several occasions during the next few months.

My wife and I also spent a lot of time with our friend, Mayra, during this same period. A major issue for Mayra was that Gilda, who was like a mother to her, suffered from Stage 4 cancer. There were little the doctors could do but try to comfort her during her remaining days.

Mayra asked me to go to Church on Sunday – December 17, 2017 – and pray for Gilda. That seemed a strange request since I assumed she knew that I was an agnostic.

Near the end of the service, I spoke to Mother Loyda about Mayra and Gilda. I said that I needed help praying and also said that I did not know which church Gilda was affiliated with. We prayed. That is when I felt a strange presence—something I never felt before. I wondered if what I felt could be God. To ask that question was to answer it.

My former self would have remarked that churches often lack sufficient heat on the coldest days. On those occasions, one can shiver even in an overcoat. The strange presence I felt was nothing like that.

What was the phenomena that I experienced called? Mayra remarked that I had been touched by an angel. A woman in my writing class said I experienced a divine awakening.

Gilda passed away a few days after I prayed with Mother Loyda. Did that mean that the Lord ignored my prayer? I discussed this with Mother Loyda and a few longstanding members of the Church. They reminded me that I previously said that the doctors could no longer do anything more than lessen the pain associated with stage 4 cancer. God ended her suffering and now she was with him. At one time, I would have ridiculed that suggestion, but looking into my head and my heart, I realized they were right.

A few months later, I visited Mother Loyda in her office. There I told her that attending Hebrew School as a youngster in the early 1960s proved a traumatic experience. The teachers as well as the rabbi constantly told students that if we were disobedient, God would punish us. I concluded that the best way to avoid God's wrath was to deny his existence. In my thirties, I realized I could not prove God's non-existence and so became an agnostic. I now wondered why it took so long for me to recognize God's existence. Mother Loyda said that is a question that only God knows the answer to.

Nina had not been actively involved with the Church. When the chorus at the Synagogue came to an end in the summer of 2018, she needed a group she could participate in. Thus, in the fall of 2018, Nina became a member of our Church's choir.

Somewhere along the line, our activities at the Church went beyond attending services on Sunday. The Church collects food scraps on Tuesday mornings (which the Sanitation Department gives to upstate farmers) and I sometimes assist the woman in charge of that program. In 2018, both Nina and I began attending Bible study on Wednesday evenings. In late December 2018 I remarked to the man who heads that program that if he predicted last year the extent of our involvement, I'd have considered that prediction preposterous.

A close relative, who is an Orthodox Jew, is not happy with our participation at the church. She feels that we should spend more time examining the richness of the religion into which we were born.

Another person unhappy about our involvement with the church is a longstanding friend from the Synagogue. Because she studied Buddhism, she should realize that everyone's path to God is different. However, she told me (in particular as opposed to both of us) that as a Jew I have no business going to Church. As she saw it, if I pray at the Church, I should stop coming to Friday night dinners at the Synagogue.

Along what path will my spiritual journey take me? I don't know.

DUE TO AN EARLY INCIDENT

Barbara Nahmias

"Due to an earlier incident in lower Manhattan, there are no downtown buses or trains running at this time," the crosstown bus driver announced.

"This won't affect me," I thought, "but it is awfully strange." Disembarking, I headed for the corner grocery store to pick up some breakfast items on the way to my office. Fruit and yogurt in hand, I approached the check-out counter, where I noticed the cashiers excitedly chattering among themselves in Spanish. "What's going on?" I asked. "A plane crashed into one of the World Trade Towers and it's on fire," they told me.

Upset, I headed for the office, hoping to catch the full story on the news. The moment I walked through the door, I heard the phone ringing off the hook. My boss, a longtime friend, had been frantically trying to call me. Before I could finish telling her what I heard at the checkout, she interrupted me. "Barbara, the trade tower that was hit has fallen and the second tower has just been hit! Close up the office, go get your kids from school and get home!" she said. "This is no accident— we are under attack!" I panicked—all I could think of was to get my family home to where, hopefully, we would all be safe, but that wasn't easy. While my 7-year-old daughter attended our neighborhood public school, my 10-year-old son attended a school for kids with special needs in Queens. All the bridges and highways had been closed and we had no way to get him. Ian also took multiple medications and I knew the school did not keep a supply on hand.

These were my racing thoughts as I sped home in a taxi. I tried to call my husband and my kids' schools but the phones were jammed. The driver had the radio tuned to the news. Five blocks from home, we heard that the second tower had fallen. I saw tears in his eyes as we both realized

45

simultaneously what this meant and my heart dropped into my stomach. "God bless you," he said as we pulled up to my door. "God help us all," I replied.

Walking into my apartment, I was relieved to see that my husband had retrieved our daughter, who was more than a little confused. How to explain to a 7-year-old without terrifying her? That would come later— and it was getting later. And still no word from our son's school. I asked my husband to stay posted by the phone while I went out to the grocery store to pick up a few things. There, I found people in a panic, buying everything in sight, literally clearing the shelves. I saw the fear in their eyes and I quickly was swept into the frenzy, loading up my own cart as if there might not be a tomorrow. Standing online to pay, I thought to myself, "What do we do now? Go empty our bank accounts?"

Home again. The doorbell rings. It's my next-door neighbor. "Ian's school called me when they could not get through to you. You had me as a secondary emergency contact. The kids are fine. They're ordering pizza for them and not letting them watch the news— but they are explaining, in very simple, basic terms, that there is an emergency that has closed the bridges and roads temporarily." I thought of these highly vulnerable children, so insecure and fearful of life as it was, dependent upon regular routines to feel safe. My heart hurt.

Some hours later, a call from another class parent. There was a plan. One of the kid's fathers, who worked for the FBI, had gathered a few other agents and was sending a caravan of cars to pick up all of the kids who lived in our area and bring them home. Incredibly, only minutes after the call, Ian, a big smile on his face, came walking through the door, accompanied by one of the agents. What would normally have been an hour and a half ride on a school bus in rush hour traffic, had taken 15 minutes on the empty roads. Speeding over the highways and bridges in a big black shiny car with his friend, sirens going full blast, had been the most thrilling experience of his life!

REMINISCING

Ravin Joseph

Sitting on the back of my neighbor's car playing click clacks waiting for our next turn in double-dutch, I hear a familiar tune. My Mr. Softee was back! I hadn't had any ice cream in a while due to him being away. My loyalty is real. I jumped off of the trunk and ran to my house, "Mommy," I shouted. She lifted the window and shouted back asking, "Are you dying?" She already knew what I wanted. She threw some change wrapped in a dollar bill from the third-floor window. I quickly caught it and ran to catch him before he made a U-turn and headed in the other direction. "Bring me back my change" she called behind me. I didn't want to make any broken promises, so I yelled, "Thank You, Mommy!" I begin to hear *Diddy's Can't Nobody Hold Me Down* in the distance. I looked towards the intersection. It was the ghetto ice cream truck turning the corner. I wondered why he would enter the block since Mr. Softee was back. I guess Mr. Softee felt the same way because he and the other guy exchanged words that were inaudible to me over the competing sounds of the trucks. The old man Mr. Softee suddenly jumped out his vehicle, bat in hand to claim his territory, driving the imposter away. *I never knew he had that in him, but then I guess we all do when the time comes,* I thought. I checked my appearance in the side-view mirror of the car. Seeing the red Kool-Aid dripping down my face and neck from my hair which I attempted to dye, I ran towards the open fire hydrant to rinse it off. Out of nowhere my brother decided to use a rusty hollow tin can to direct the blasting water towards me. I was soaked, my hair began to shrivel, and my sandals felt like jelly when I walked.

Annoyed, I silently plotted on how I was going to retaliate as I yelled over to my best friend Tammy. Together, we began to walk to the local corner store, Benny's. I could only go to Benny's because my mom didn't want me hanging out on Cozy Corner, which was in the opposite direction and so much closer. It was Friday and TGIF was coming on soon. Last night I had gotten my tail whipped for staying out past curfew. I was playing Manhunt with my brother and his friends on the block and lost track of time. *Why couldn't my mom just let me stay out until the streetlights came on like most parents and why didn't my brother get licks too? I am so much more mature than he is,* I thought. I was just grateful to be able to go back outside so soon, so I didn't complain aloud. My backside was still sore and was a reminder to bring in my tail on time tonight. When we arrived at the corner store, I grabbed two ice cream sandwiches out of the freezer before asking for a pack of Winterfresh gum, box of Boston Baked Beans, and two packs of sunflower seeds that were sitting behind the counter. I paid and waited for Tammy outside.

As we walked back, we decided to make a pit stop, where I found the black mark on the inside of the gum wrapper. I had Tammy break it with me. I called out the letters of the alphabet as I fingered through the letters on the wrapper. "A B C D E ..." I stopped at "P" although there were more symbols left to go. "Parker" my best friend teased. I knew even if I landed on another letter at the end of the day, Parker would be my future husband, so why would I care about the ones before. Parker usually hung out at the basketball court at Soundview Park known to us as the "Jungle". I grew excited about seeing him. We were the original Monica and Quincy before Love and Basketball. I mean, we never made it on the court, but in my head, we took home the chip. As we walked up to the Jungle, Tammy did a quick scan and responded "Negative." The OG's were out on the court arguing over a call, talking their shit as usual. We decided to take the shortcut through the woods to my house located behind the Jungle. As I walked closer, I could see my mom looking out the window. *It's not even 8:00 yet,* I thought. "She be beastin" I said as I rolled my eyes too far away for her to notice. As soon as my big toe touched the street she yelled: "Come inside Tifi". "I was," I snapped. My mom always had to remind me of how much freedom I did have. She was from the Island of St. Lucia and

48

her father being a 7-Day Adventist, kept her and her siblings on a tight leash. I imagine my mom with her almond-shaped eyes, mean walk, slim body, gorgeous smile, and mesmerizing charm lived in a small room where only sunlight could sneak through. She probably just read and took care of her ten other siblings. I imagine she tried hard to please her dad, waking up at 4 am to help at his bakery to then go to school, come home and being exhausted still have the responsibility of cooking and doing homework. I imagine that one day, while my mom sat in meditation on the shore of Laborie beach, my grandmother's spirit spoke to her giving her the courage to run away and obtain her freedom, to be whom she wanted to be, not what was expected of her. Either that or she met a guy. She had been helping to raise her siblings since she was eleven. She deserved to be her own woman.

I invited Tammy to come upstairs with me, but she declined. As many times as I had extended the invitation, she never accepted it. I hugged her barely. She was awkward when it came to those things. As soon as I got upstairs, my mother told me to take my clothes off and get into the bathtub. I could hear Wheel of Fortune on in the background as she checked my body and hair for ticks. "You want your hair to fall out?" she asked before telling me to rinse my hair of the Kool-Aid. "Where is your jump rope?" she asked. "I brung it in earlier," I said. "Brung is not a word. It's *brought*. I told you about bringing that street talk into my house already." I rolled my eyes. She caught me in the reflection of the mirror and pulled the scarf tighter cutting off the circulation to my brain as she tied my hair for bed.

I headed to the kitchen after putting on my favorite Rugrats nighty. My junk food replaced with provisions and fish sat covered on the kitchen table. With my brother already seated at the table, my mom made me say grace before we ate. We bowed our heads and closed our eyes. I shared aloud, "Dear Lord, please bless this food we are about to receive, thank you for giving mommy the strength to prepare it. May it nourish our bodies. Amen". I looked up and noticed my brother looking at me, smiling. Before I could even guess what was on his mind, he picked out the fisheye and showed it to me before he popped it into his mouth. Of course, being that I want to be just like him, I had to suck up any disgust that I felt and follow suit. "Mal Pwopte" Mommy shouts in creole as I felt the slimy object move towards the back of my throat. She always called us nasty. That's our thing, that's how we bond, my brother and I. We are a year and a half apart and always competing. My brother laughed and pointed at my facial expression which I quickly turned into a smile.

Saturday mornings were for family outings. We went to Shorehaven for a picnic and to catch crabs. On the way back, I saw my godmother outside filling up her super soaker. They were too expensive for my mom to afford, but my godmother, having two, allowed me to borrow one. I went into her garage and quickly filled the container with water. I was planning a sneak attack. I climbed the tree in front of my godmother's house and patiently waited for my brother to pass by. I could see him walking up the block with mommy. I pumped the super soaker and took aim. When he grew closer, I pressed my finger on the trigger with all my might, soaking his clothing. "Got you!" I yelled. Pleased with my success, I laughed out loud. He wasn't too happy because he was wearing his white Air force One sneakers. "Imma catch you, watch" he said, shaking out his t-shirt. Mommy laughed too. She knew the struggle I faced trying to fit in with the guys. *No remorse,* I thought as we walked home.

Like any Sunday, we woke up and got dressed to head to service at Holy Cross. We had arrived at the afternoon mass and it was packed and full of life. My family always sat together at the second to the last pew on the far right of the church. I wondered to myself if mommy heard of the Rosa Parks story. "A family that prays together stays together" she repeatedly told my brother and I. Dante was on guitar and my favorite choir singer Adriana was there to sing the "Amen" hymn I loved so much. She was the local Mariah Carey. At the altar was a painting of a white man who looked like he was levitating in front of the sun. We learned that a nun from the early 1900s saw Christ and after recording her encounters, created this image. Christ was white. The white man saved us, I learned. After leaving mass, I walked over to purchase some flowers for mommy's kitchen table. We weren't allowed to watch tv until after 6 pm on Sundays so when we finally arrived home, before taking off my shoes, I asked "Can I please go outside?" "Outside has nothing but trouble" my mother voiced, "Go and find a book to read." I rolled my eyes, this time making sure she couldn't see me.

I grabbed a book off the shelf and jumped onto the top bunk. I quickly became engrossed in *The Baby-Sitters Club Little Sister* series no.11. It was two hours later when I finally looked up and snapped back to reality. I enjoyed reading, but I needed to see Parker before it became too late. I hadn't seen him in days and was going through withdrawals, or so I thought. I made the excuse of having to walk our dog Ori so I would be allowed to go outside. I walked up to the Jungle and noticed Parker was out balling with the fellas. It was Jungle Sunday. It was routine for guys from the neighborhood to be here each week. I walked into the park just as a game was finishing. Parker walked toward a white girl standing on the sideline and kissed her. The fellas made sounds teasing him. I was heartbroken. *The guys I like seem to find interest in the light-skinned girls,* I thought. I had learned this lesson in the third grade.

I walked Ori home. He quickly ran up the stairs and scratched on the door for mommy to open it. I carefully snuck back outside. I'd deal with the repercussions later. I ran over to Tammy's house to fill her in on what had happened. I needed consoling. I rang the doorbell repeatedly but no answer. She was a homebody. I just knew she was home. Finally, her mom opened the door. "Hey Burtena, Tammy is sleeping right now. I'll tell her you stopped by" she stated. "Ok, Ms. Carmen, thanks." I replied. I looked up at the window as I walked away and caught a glimpse of the bracelet I gave Tammy for her last birthday, before her hand disappeared behind the curtain. I never saw Tammy again.

PRESS AND CURL

Marie Daugherty

Growing up in the South Bronx during the depression, the big one during the 1930s, my mother was forced to learn skills that would stay with her for a lifetime. There was no money for things people now take for granted like store bought clothes, restaurant meals or the hairdresser. Dreadlocks, Afros, Bantu knots and two stranded twists were unknown. Women washed and styled their hair at home. If worn natural, the hair would often be parted and braided with black bobby pins strategically placed to give the hair a close to the head profile with a hat or scarf as cover. The other choice was to press and curl.

Because she was the third daughter, my mother was fourth in line to have her hair done. My grandmother would wash and press her hair first. She would take care of her daughters always starting with the oldest first. Lil, the oldest would towel dry her shampooed hair while DD was being washed. Mommy was last. The same order was followed for straightening hair. After three heads, Mommy's hair wouldn't be straightened although she pleaded with my grandmother. A variety of reasons were given. There isn't enough time. You too young. I don't have time cause I have to fix supper for your father. Your hair don't need no straightening.

After weeks of disappointment, Mommy asked for permission to use the pressing comb to do her own hair. Although Mommy was just 12 years old, my grandmother gave her the iron. She knew that if she didn't straighten her hair, it would never get done. She didn't know when the comb was too hot or not hot enough. When the too hot comb singed her hair, my grandmother would laugh. "You burnin' you hair. You gonna end up bald." When my mother was perceived as taking too long at the stove, "Hurry up! I got to use the stove to cook for your father. Make sure the pilot light don't go out. Don't want this house exploding."

Many years later, by the time I was entering school, Mommy had perfected her pressing technique. Although the big depression had passed, we were experiencing a small one. We still sewed most of our clothes at home. Occasionally on payday, there might be a treat of take-out from the local Chinese restaurant. Hair was still cared for at home. Mommy would press, curl and style my grandmother's hair for special occasions like Easter, a wedding, a funeral, a christening or baptism. She was happy to practice a skill she had perfected without my grandmother's help.

I started school in a new neighborhood. We had move to the east side of the Bronx River because NYC had decided to demolish the old apartment buildings where we lived and replace them with modern housing projects. We lived in a project built on vacant land. The school was integrated; the classes were not. I was placed in a class filled with white students because the other class, with blacks (called colored), Puerto Ricans and poor whites (I assumed later they were poor although no one was well of) had reached its capacity.

Mommy began to straighten my hair when I was 7 or 8 despite the disapproval of my grandmother who insisted "Chillen that age don't need no hot comb." Saturdays or Sunday mornings or afternoons or whenever time could be found between grocery shopping or household chores, I would sit on a step ladder chair to the left of the stove facing the window, often still in my two-piece footie pajamas. An open can of Apex pressing oil sat on the sink cover several inches from the flame which heated the steel hot comb. Mommy would part my hair into small sections, applying a tiny amount of the Apex to each section while the pressing comb heated in the flame. She tested the temperature of the comb on an old folded towel. If it was too hot, she would place it on the stove away from the flame and fan it to cool it quickly. I could feel my mother's warm breath as she blew on the comb as she pulled it through my hair. After she finished, she would divide my hair into 5 braids or twists. As I grew older, I wore 3 braids because I felt that 5 was too much.

In sixth grade, I no longer wanted to wear my hair braided. Maybe it was one too many comments or questions about my hair from students in my class. I was still the black girl in the mainly white class. I asked Mommy if I could wear my hair loose and have it curled. My normally strict mother eventually agreed. My hair was cut in a curled bang with a flip in the back.

My grandmother complained that, "children were supposed to wear their hair in braids." My mother told my grandmother that she didn't want me feeling different, standing out in that white school. A few of the black girls in the other class looked at me with a surprised look on their faces. I could only guess what they were thinking. I was proud that my mother stood up to my grandmother. However, no amount of press and curl could prevent me from standing out in class.

CONNECTIONS

Debra Bramlett

I've always been a spirit connected to the Universe. Recognizing this connection at an early age, I've thought of it as "something said to me!" Most often, I would hear and act upon the guidance. Miss Jones, an elderly neighbor, was a good friend of mine when I was growing up in St. Louis. Mo., in the 1960's. That "something" used to say "time to go see Miss Jones" and I would stop playing with the other children to go visit her right at that very moment! I remember when Lamont, a neighborhood playmate who was about 10 at the time, said "Why do you go see that old lady?" And I being about 8, declared "because she's my friend!"

Our connections run deep, like roots in the ground, spreading to an emotional and physical embodiment in ways we can't always envision. That's what I learned through a true-life altering experience at the age of 53 with 3 children (Michael, Nelson, Jessica) and my husband Dwayne of twenty-five years. My sixth sense didn't just show up, but I was about to find out how deeply it flowed!

My first glimpse came in December 2009 as I walked from the bedroom to the kitchen in our home in downtown Brooklyn. That "something" said "three strikes and you're out!" Suddenly a quiver of fear raced through my entire being. I took note, not really understanding what it meant!   Two weeks later I suggested to my middle child Nelson who was home on college winter break, that I wanted to buy him a pair of boots. He declined because his Auntie Gail had already ordered him a pair and they would be arriving soon. "Well it's alright to have two pairs" I chuckled; "no thanks" he replied. Nelson didn't want a lot of clothes or shoes, but his sister sure did!

On New Years' day, January 2010 Nelson broke his ankle, slipping on black ice as he returned to his friend Jesse's apartment in the wee hours of the morning. Once I found out about Nelson's accident, I became quite fearful. A few years before he had stitches on a gash on his left finger, then he had to have minor surgery on his ankle. I was very concerned that any other injury would be a third strike out - I could not be sure at first who could be in danger!

Like a zoom camera my focus went straight on to him. Returning to school after his winter break on crutches was not ideal, since his campus in Rochester, NY, was really snowed in. But thanks to help from his roommate Dan, he made it through to a sunny spring with a successful cast removal.

I still felt shaky, but the intensity had lessened, and life seemed to be moving nicely. It's May 2010 and Nelson is back home after finishing his 3rd year at the University. Jessica returned the following week after completing her first year of college in Boston. We got to kick off the summer at a family Bar-B-Que in Crown Heights and all was good.

Wow, the summer flew by fast; it was July already! I was so thankful both Jess and Nelson got summer jobs. I had just returned home from a three week visit with my big sister Gail, who lives in the Detroit, MI, area. Nelson sweet talked me, smiling he pleaded "make me a St. Paul sandwich Mommy?" I happily cooed "I am in full Mommy mode until you guys go back to school!" That meant pancakes, banana pudding, fried green tomatoes and anything else in reason. I was prepared to throw down, if the weather would allow it.

New York City experienced an extreme heat wave, July 22nd through the 24th, which helped make the summer of 2010 one of the hottest on record! That Friday morning, July 23rd, was so beautiful. We made plans to go shopping near 34th Street in Manhattan and also to enjoy the air conditioning which was really needed. After doing some shopping at Macy's, Jess departed for her salon appointment. Nelson and I headed over to J.C. Penny's and shared some quality moments. Using my coupon savvy, he was able to pick out a few outfits of his style and liking. Returning home, we rested then headed out to do grocery shopping at the Key Food on

Fifth Avenue. Ooh how Nelson loved to eat his Mom's cooking, all of my kids did; but Nelson had been my grocery shopping partner since his middle school years.

Saturday Morning was delightful as I sipped coffee in our backyard while the chirping birds serenaded me. I started preparing brunch knowing that soon after eating, everyone would scatter. Dwayne headed off to his waiter's nightshift at the Italian Restaurant where he worked in Park Slope. Nelson had errands to run and would come back in a bit. Jessica had plans for a girls' night out/sleepover at her BFF's Remi's Bed-Stuy home. That left me cleaning up the kitchen and completing my chore list for the day. Chillin' in the living room with both front and back doors wide open to receive any breeze that did come by, I was relaxed. Of course, having iron screen gated doors added to my peace of mind!

Returning a couple of hours later Nelson grinned, using his "Please, please Mommy voice", and asked "Will you oil and trim my locks?" "Sure, I will baby, it's my pleasure!" We used to be a family with locks and Nelson was our only child who kept his. He sat between my legs as I worked on his hair. This labor of love was mine, our precious bonding time together! We chatted about school, girls, safe sex, future meals and hanging out at the beach. After he gave approval for a job well done, Nelson bopped down the stairs to his cool and comfortable bedroom in the basement. Soon he would return to Rochester Institute of Technology for fall semester. I missed my babies while they were away, and I treasured all the time I could get.

Checking in with him an hour later, I inquired about his possible evening plans: 1) party with friends in Manhattan, 2) College buddy birthday pool party on Long Island or 3) chill in the basement. "Cool" I shouted, "If you decide to stay, we can order sushi delivery later." Hopping up each step, Nelson announced "Made my decision Mom!" "Peeps keep blowin' up my phone; I'm headed to the pool party." "So, how will you get to the house from the train station?" "Will there be any real adults there?" He responded, "Yes, Jeff will pick me up and his parents are at the house." "Hmm, I don't want him driving you after partying." "Are others spending the night?" "A few," he answered. "Well listen, I want to speak to the mother, because I got that "feeling" I told you about." "Dang Mom, don't be ridiculous," he said slightly annoyed. But "I'll call if you want." "I want," leaning over kissing his cheek.

Introducing myself, I point blank asked the mother, "Will there be mature adult supervision?" and "Will there be a lot of heavy drinking going on?" Immediately, flashes of CSI Miami pool party tragedies darted through my mind. "No Mommy, it's not that kind of party!" she assured me.

"No more than two drinks, remember to eat, drink plenty of water, it's 100 degrees and climbing, use sunscreen and stay away from the deep end!" I stated. "Yeah, hey, what, what, I have you know I have five years of swimming competitions under my belt!" he boasted. "I know, I took you to the lessons. Ok, so just be careful." We kissed and hugged goodbye as he rushed out to catch the 4:10 departing from Atlantic Terminal. "Safe and sound," he happily shouted from a loud party atmosphere background, "see ya tomorrow." I hung up with no apprehensions. Eating a snack, I began to feel that "something" again. But soon after that, I received a text with a heart from him and my anxiety eased.

The stickiness alone made it hard to breath, so sitting up to 4:00 in the morning watching a movie worked out perfectly for us. Abruptly I blurted out, "that sounds like Nelson coming in." And my husband responded, rolling his eyes, "I didn't hear anything." Without warning, a piercing fear ripped through my senses like a fierce storm! It felt to me like Nelson was staggering and gulping for breath, driving me to clutch myself in terror! Springing from the couch, I stepped into the foyer gazing out the screen door to check for myself; then, I had my husband go to the front yard to look up and down our block. "Didn't see him; he's alright; he's twenty-one; stop worrying," he reassuringly stated. I agreed to calm down, as I prepared for bed, even though I was still scared.

The stark silence was ruptured by the call no parent ever wants to receive! Dwayne jumped up answering the house phone which seldom rang. "Yes, this is he, what, what did you say," his answers dripping in a thick, painfully excruciating pitch! In this tiny voice I asked, "Is it Nelson?" "Yes," he cried out in agony! I was numb. Redialing the number, I had to hear the doctor say that our Nelson Douglas Cole, my baby, our baby was gone! That confirmed to me Nelson's SPIRIT had come back home! Dwayne called our long-time friends Michele and Lenny and broke the horrible news. They came to drive us out to Long Island to claim our Nelson. Jumping into their car in a state of shock, we turned the corner on to Bond St. heading for the BQE expressway. Dwayne screamed "Stop! There's Jess coming down the street." Then Lenny pulled over. That "something" had her come home around 7:30 a.m. which we were grateful for. Therefore, she did not have to return to an empty home. This allowed her to hear the sorrowful news in person and make the journey with us to begin the final act of goodbye!

It's hard to believe how Sunday July 25, 2010, the worst day of our lives also represented, for me, a new era of deep consciousness and metaphysical experiences. As a result, my mind opened up in ways I could not have fathomed. Nelson visited his sister and me leaving messages of empowerment that night! He said to me, "Let's do this thang." I awakened the next day with a plan and directions from Nelson as to how his farewell celebration should flow, secure in the knowledge that we would always be CONNECTED!

THROUGH THE JOURNEY

Arlene Crystal Santiago

From the moment we enter this beautiful world, we are born with incredible perseverance and responsibility. Most women juggle motherhood, their jobs and normal life duties, yet must be efficient at multitasking. We're expected to live a lucrative life filled with hard work and sacrifices, but at times we also receive unwelcomed challenges.

Some of those challenges within my journey was being diagnosed with cancer; not once, but 5 times. Oh, the magical number 5, like the song "mambo number 5". Some days it would feel as if my life was a wild dance with cancer.

In those many battles that I had, I felt as if I had lost everything that made me a woman. They removed my breasts, ovaries and my womb—all gone in the name of staying alive and you know, to enhance my quality of living.

"Why are you happy and grateful with all this unfortunate juncture, aren't you in an aggro state of mind?" they would ask me. My response was always "No, I'm not unhappy with how my life has played out." I stopped questioning the reason or the purpose of what is taking place within my body. I am learning to gracefully welcome the changes. I understand that this walk is not easy, but I'm learning patience. I'm learning to embrace the courage that is inside of me and to spread that light / positivity to others who may be in need. Life is chaotic, and there are many factors that can bring someone down—it's not just cancer.

During my battle with breast cancer, I was given four years to live. I decided to start taking as many photos of my family as I could so they could remember the moments we shared together. Eventually, the photographs started growing into something more and I began to take pictures of my surroundings, and things that inspired me. As the creative side that never existed before was born, I began to look into this magical lens that captured true life events, breathtaking plants, flowers, and moments that would be gone forever if not captured.

I choose to be a beacon of hope for all those who are in the midst of difficulty. To show them that living and existing is beautiful and that each life is worth fighting for. The love and support of families, friends and even beloved pets are vital within the healing process. It is also necessary to find inspiration in the midst of the good fight.

For me, photography had opened the door for self-discovery and has given me a profound love of all the beauty that surrounds me. Photography was the creative outlet that helped save my life. It helped me remove any negative thoughts and allowed me to focus on the things that brought me joy. For anyone battling cancer I would try to encourage them to open up a new sense of creativity, such as writing, drawing, painting, singing, photography or anything that inspires you. Learn to turn the pain into positivity and allow that pain, suffering and the challenges you've faced to flourish into a new air of peace and prosperity. Allow yourself to grow and expand in a beautiful way... Flourish, baby. Flourish.

PRAYING

Sarah Ann Smith

As far as I can remember, my mother got on her knees each night to pray. By her side of the bed, my mother kneeled, offering thanks for the gifts of her husband, her children, and her home. Using dish washed hands to give her leverage to push herself off the floor, my mother would then lay beside the safety and warmth of her husband.

My mother prayed every night for the blessings of my father: a tall, skinny, handsome man, who worked hard, and loved God and family. Strong silent prayers that spoke loudly of her relationship with God. My father's prayers could be heard in the humming and singing he did on Sunday mornings, in communication with God as he baked. You could taste his thankfulness in the sweetness of his homemade cakes, breads, and pies. These were offerings, a gift for his family and friends. His daily actions taught us to give thanks for the past week, having made it, or still making it through whatever came our way, and to give thanks for the blessings of God's grace in the midst of the mystery of the week to come.

My mother considered herself big, a housewife, who bore my father 5 children. I thought my mother to be pleasantly plump, how a mother should feel, soft, with goodness. She was not a big eater. She was just a woman who cooked full meals every day, who spent her day cooking, cleaning, washing and taking care of her children and home. Yet, with no regard to her size, or the tiredness from her day, my mother kneeled every night in prayer.

Sadly now, I don't ever remember getting down on my own knees to pray beside her. I guess because I always had a room space or bed of my own. Even now, it is not something I do often, maybe in a moment of deep distress. To tell the truth, either my knees start hurting, or I start falling asleep, and

I rush through the prayer. But my mother, my mother never complained about her knees, or the effort it took to get down and up...even as she grew older.

My daughter, just turned 30, spent a lot of time with my mother over the years, as a baby, and little girl. She often slept in the same bed, after the death of my father. And now, 20 years after the death of my mother, my daughter still kneels in prayer every night. My daughter gives thanks for all of her loved ones, sending prayers to heaven for all of her angels. She keeps my mother's bedtime tradition, even when she occasionally sleeps with me, for a night of comfort through sad anniversaries or birthdays. Her need to be near me, her Momma. Her feelings of safety and love in her mother's bed. It is me, the one my daughter now prays for the most. I endure her in my space, cutting down the volume on my tv, shushing me with her finger, quieting me with a look, if I forget, and start to say something before she finishes her silent prayers.

And though I haven't yet knelt beside her, I have taken her hand in mine, not just at night, but in various places, in serious times, and asked her to pray with me. And I can picture my mother kneeling and hear my father humming. "Our father, who art in heaven...."

THE BOYS ON THE STOOP

Harriet Bailer

795 East 179th Street in the Bronx was a great place for boys to grow up. There was Peter, as well as Norman, who had two brothers, and Brucie, also with two brother siblings.

As for me, I was about 11 or 12 years old, and I was the only girl in the apartment building, with no friends except Anise who lived about 100 feet down the block. Anise's father used a separate entrance in my building, though he wasn't the super. Oh, and I must mention Anise's strange brother. We knew nothing about him, not even his name!

The boys played in the streets, all summer long. Ring-a-levio, stick ball, and kings were some of their games. Meanwhile, the boys taught me to play chess. I wasn't very good at it, but nevertheless I became one of the boys on the concrete steps of 795.

We played all day, long after the sunset. I couldn't wait until the next day.

WATERBURY PARK

Ed Friedman

It was the beginning of the end.

I was a very young twenty-two-year-old and was about to marry my second serious girlfriend and the only woman I'd ever had sex with. All of this seemed perfectly normal. It was 1971 in the East Bronx and getting married young was what we did. It was what we did when we weren't drinking, playing cards, gambling with bookmakers, going to the track or playing ball. For most of us marriage would be a blip in our lives. With the exception of having to go to a "job" (no one ever used the word "career") life would go on as it had. Not much would change except that sex was a given and only those most desperate to flaunt their vows would continue to visit the prostitutes on Simpson Street.

It was clear to me that I would be deviating from this pattern. I was too analytical and introspective to continue this extended adolescence. I spent too much time thinking about the feelings of my young wife-to-be. I started taking night courses at a community college. None of this was revealed to my friends as I continued to act as if my life was completely untethered. I knew that in a week's time I would be different —I would be married and with that vow I would make a seismic shift to a more responsible life. Until then I would live as though a switch would come on the moment I said, "I do".

It's with that complete confidence in how my life would go forward that I sat in the back seat of Ralph DiNardo's father's Ford with five other young men, none with a serious thought among them. All of them taking for granted that they would live forever; a bottle of vodka mixed with Tropicana fueling their feeling of invincibility. The local bars being populated by old men who were veteran drinkers and listeners of Frank Sinatra. We preferred the Ford as a lounge on wheels where we could turn up the Three Dog Night, or The Temptations. On this day, Joe, eldest of the group and the only one sporting facial hair opened up a large brown bag, the contents of which made up the solid food portion of our cocktail hour.

"I wanted barbecue, Where's the barbecue chips?" Louis piped up.

"They're at the store, right under the ones that taste good," Frankie responded.

"Eat shit and die," which was our comeback de jour.

"That's what I woulda done if I got those barbecue chips. Besides, nobody likes them but you." Joe opened the bag of "regular" potato chips, stuck his hand in the bag, pulled out an outsize handful and began eating them.

Though this strikes all of us as absurd, only Louis speaks up. "So whadda think, if we finish those right away we'll go out and get barbecue?"

"Get outta here."

Louis, defensive, retorted, "Hey I chipped in."

"You want your money back?" Joe is reaching into his pocket in the name of justice and to get Louis to shut up. This works, as Louis refuses the money and therefore gives up any moral high ground. Assuming there is a moral high ground in the discussion of salted snacks.

The car was parked right at the entrance to Waterbury Park. The park sits on a square block surrounded by a fence. The entrance opens up to handball courts, a large baseball field, and beyond the field a children's playground. Ringing the park are neatly kept one-family homes, either attached or semi-attached. It's a working-class neighborhood made up largely of second generation Italian-Americans who took great pride at leaving East Harlem apartments for their own homes in the Bronx. It was the kind of place you could always feel safe. That feeling of safety in your own park is probably why I don't notice the three cars pull up in front, behind and next to the Ford. I watch a parade of young men spring out of the cars like clowns emerging from a Volkswagen on an old TV commercial. I'm not putting together what's going on and trying to look in all directions when I feel a metal cylinder pressed hard against my head through the open window. The cylinder is the barrel of a gun being held by someone telling me to "Get the fuck outta the car". I turn my head and all I see is the barrel. I'm aware that my friends are all facing the same threats.

Those who don't move fast enough are dragged out of the car and all of us are thrown against the fence to face our attackers most of whom have baseball bats. A few others have knives. Although it's not at my head anymore I can't take my eyes off the gun.

We're all silent. It's a strange amalgam of being too scared to say anything and too proud to beg for your life. And now I'm thinking I'm going to die a week before my wedding. My mind darts to Roseann and remember she's only twenty. Once the tragedy wears off, she'll be dating again and probably married in a year. Eventually I'll just be an interesting footnote in her life. When the story is told at parties I won't even be the main character. It will be all about how Roseann dealt with my death.

I am paralyzed with silence and can now no longer look at the gun because I'm afraid somehow if I look at it, it will go off. We're being cursed at and our manhoods insulted but nobody is shooting or stabbing yet. We're trapped and it occurs to me that this could end peacefully or with one flinch we could all be dead. Our looks of incredulity are visible to some of our attackers, one of whom feels compelled to give us the cause for this attack.

"Paulie's brother got jumped and somebody said that the guys who did it hang out at Waterbury Park."

Stevie, who five minutes before was playing air guitar in the front seat blurts out, "who the hell is his brother?" The leader's bat connects with Stevie's head. The gang looks at us waiting for our reaction. Somehow there's a collective consciousness and we remain frozen. We all know if we make one move it's all over.

The next five seconds take forever to pass.

Joe finally speaks. "Not for nuthin, but bring your brother over, he'll tell you it wasn't us". The leader motions to one of his group who disappears into one of the cars. He comes back with a frightened sixteen-year-old who takes a look at us and shakes his head. The leader motions to his group who pile back into their cars and screech away from the park. We go to Stevie and luckily he's not really hurt. No one spoke for a few minutes. There was a time when retaliation would have been just moments away. But as we collected ourselves and realized how close we came to being a tragic headline, there was a palpable awareness of the lifting of our assumed invincibility.

It was the beginning of the end.

AFRAID TO PEE & MY DEER MOMENT

Henry Torres

When we were very young my siblings and I would crowd around our maternal grandmother to hear her tell stories of what life was like when she was a young girl living in Puerto Rico this inspired me to write these pieces. 'Abuela' always started her stories with the phrase: 'en los tiempos de antes' (in the old days) now it's my turn to tell stories of what it was like when I was young living in the lower east side of New York City— in stream of consciousness form.

---

*en los tiempos de antes...*mami would send me off to sleep-away Camp Wabenaki the first two weeks in July after she frugally spent her little bit of cash to buy camp supplies I needed from the standard camp list and on the designated departure day would walk me down 3rd Street to the Boys Brotherhood Republic (BBR) clubhouse to catch a Campus bus with many other fellow campers onto which we were instructed to sing camp songs like *Into the Air Junior Birdman* & *We are The Boys of BBR You Hear So Much About* as well as *...all those bottles of beer on the wall* and many more since being an extremely shy person I only mouthed and when the bus reached camp two hours away in upstate New York we were escorted off to pick up our luggage which had been lined-up on a dirt path then we were taken to the mess hall and informed of what Indian tribe we were assigned to for the duration of our two week stay and this time I was a Mohawk and with the rest of the Mohawk braves we were escorted to our sleeping quarters inside a canvas tent that housed ten metal spring bunk beds that ran along the inside and we were instructed to stow our belongings in the foot lockers near the beds and told the camp rules by our counselor then shown where the latrines were which scared me because I was so shy to have to expose myself while both peeing and doing number 2 as well as showering since the showers were in the same location and it smelled but I have to admit that taking a tingle or a dump was weirdly fun because the pee or poop dropped splashed & echoed after hitting the dirty water below and during the day we were allowed a half hour of free time and here's when I came across a really cool experience reminding me of when the Gordie character in *"Stand by Me"* saw a deer near the railroad tracks and this was way before the movie came out so I lay claim to the experience which happened when I went off to an isolated spot on the outskirts of the camp to get away from having to relate with anyone and enjoy a few moments of solitude is when I saw something moving ahead of me and realized it was a deer who perhaps might also have been trying to find some solace and while after turning its head in my direction it allowed me to approach almost as if wanting to ask my name while the moment extended itself and we stared into each other's eyes I was frozen in the holiness of the situation before the spell was broken when the deer fled as the camp signal was given that free time was over I decided to keep my special moment a secret and told no one of my mystical encounter

WHY DO I HAVE TO GO UPSTAIRS?

Mindy Matijasevic

My mother came down, her coat over her nightgown, to tell me I had to come upstairs. I was in the middle of a game of Captain with other kids from the building. It was a game similar to handball. It wasn't time for me to be home, and my mother never did this. Something wasn't right.

My mother didn't give me any reason though I kept asking her why as we rode up in the elevator. That wasn't like her. Inside the apartment, my teenage aunt was holding a steak knife to my grandmother. It could have been about wanting money for clothes. I didn't know how it began. I stood inside by the apartment door. I stared horrified at the knife near my grandma's neck. She stared at her youngest daughter. Grandma didn't look scared. I didn't understand that. I thought maybe she was pretending not to be scared.

I kept thinking I needed to run out and ask a neighbor to call the police, but I knew Grandma would be so mad at me for letting anyone know what was going on. I feared she'd put me in a foster home like she often threatened to do, and I'd never see my mother or grandparents again. But if my aunt killed Grandma, and I didn't try to get help, I would not be able to go on living. I knew that.

I felt paralyzed. I couldn't believe my aunt would use the knife on her own mother, but my aunt *was* a violent person. I had always known her that way. How long do I wait? I loved Grandma, but I also knew she would be angrier at me for telling than at my aunt for holding a knife to her.

I couldn't understand why my mother had insisted I come upstairs. What was *I* supposed to do? My aunt was ten years older than me and dangerous. I was afraid of her. Minutes earlier, I was with kids who would be spared from this kind of thing and whose main concern was hitting the Spalding ball against the brick building. They'd never imagine why I was made to go upstairs. They'd never know how lucky they were. I had been playing with them as if I had the right to be a kid, but I didn't.

Eventually, my aunt said, "If I didn't have to go to jail, I wouldn't think twice." She put the knife down.

MUSING OF A NURSE ON A HOT SUMMER DAY, 1987

Alice Myerson

The windows are nailed shut, and the room is stifling. "Too many break-ins," he had said. "They come down from the roof."

We have been sitting at his dining room table for almost two hours now, Mr. Johnson and I, waiting for the medicine to bring down his blood pressure. "200/110," I said when I came in, "too high." "The hospital," he said, shaking his head emphatically, "no, not again. Too many white coats."

It is a no that I am just beginning to appreciate. Nursing in the community is not the same as nursing in the hospital. In the community, I make no pretense of control. My attention has changed. I negotiate my way through dark rooms, roaches and mice. No more sterile walls and frenetic codes. My focus has deepened in these rooms. I tend to the details of the body and discover the person who lives in that body. Healing takes place when I touch a soul with kindness. But kindness without knowledge will not heal. That I have always known. But knowledge gives us choice, and I am learning to accept that the choices I offer are not mine to make. That is new to me.

The room tells his story. Three white kitchen cabinets filled with white paper bags. The bags are filled with unopened bottles of pills. A refrigerator with a pitcher of water and three eggs. One solitary chrome plated basketball trophy on a glass shelf in a display cabinet in the far corner of the living room. Naked floors. Paint chips and the outline of a frame where a picture once hung. There was laughter here once, before he faded into the curtain of alone.

He worked, oh, years ago, he told me, in a factory on Canal, and his eyes brightened, but the Social Security money doesn't go far, what with all the medicine the doctor gives him, the pink pills, the big white pills, and the little ones, and the blue capsules. "Which ones do you take?" I asked. "Well, in the morning, it's the pink pill," and he studied the bottle in his hand, and I realized the letters on the labels were incomprehensible to him.

I check my work. I have replaced the bottles of unopened pills in their white paper bags and returned them to the shelves inside the kitchen cabinets. I have given him water and replenished the water pitcher. I have labeled two paper cups with adhesive tape, one with the moon, the other with the sun. Each cup contains the pills for evening and for morning, and the cups are neatly placed next to the empty glass on the dining room table. Everything is set.

I wrap the blood pressure cuff around his wasted bicep and place my stethoscope on the crook of his arm. I pump up the machine and listen carefully for his heart to speak and to be heard. The thready feel of a failing pulse is replaced by the firm beat of a healing heart.

"150 over 92," I say quietly. "Much better now. And the funny feeling in your eyes? Is it gone?"

Mr. Johnson nods.

I fold up my machine, take the stethoscope from my neck, put them back in my nursing bag. I squeeze alcohol over my hands, rub them together, zip up the bag, lift it off the dining room table and throw it over my left shoulder.

"I'll be going now," I say.

Mr. Johnson follows me, steadied by his cane. "Sorry, Nurse, to take up so much time."

"No worries," I say, gently touching his sleeve. "My other patients will understand. And don't forget to take the blue pill in the cup marked with the moon tonight. Take the two white pills tomorrow morning from the cup marked with the sun. I'll be back around 10:30 to check on you. I'll bring you a pill box to fix your medicines. You'll see. We'll get it all straightened out."

And then, remembering the refrigerator with three eggs, I say, "Oh, and you're sure your neighbor will bring you some dinner?"

Mr. Johnson nods his head. "Thank you, Nurse," he says. "I'll be just fine." And he slides the police lock along its track and opens the door.

"Tomorrow then." I step across the saddle of the door. Three clicks, three locks and the door is secured behind me.

Not even a crumb for the roaches.

New prescriptions with each visit to the ER or the clinic. Food or medicine. What kind of a choice is that? Bottles of pills with labels he can't read. I shake my head in disbelief.

The elevator to the sixth floor where I wait is taking its time. I check my watch and shuffle my feet impatiently. The elevator finally comes and its door slides open. I am about to step into it but the smell repels me. Bile surges through my throat and reaches for the back of my tongue. Flies swarm around a plastic bag filled with rotting garbage abandoned in the corner of the tiny car. The stench is overwhelming.

"Shit, I guess I'll have to walk."

The weight of my bag, the smell of the garbage, the oppressive heat and the gurgle in my belly, it is all so heavy, and I swoon under its weight. I grab the banister. My palms stick to the wooden railing as I make my way down the worn stairs, past the broken windows and the graffitied walls. I stop on each landing to catch my breath, to search for the eyes I do not see, the voices I do not hear, the echo of footsteps that can only be my own.

From the first-floor landing, I see water drip from the ceiling of the lobby into metal buckets placed strategically on the lobby floor. There is a rustling under me. I look into a haze of smoke that smells like burnt plastic mixed with skunk.

Crack. Under the stairwell.

I take a deep breath. I hurry down the last set of stairs, weave around the buckets and push open the front door.

Outside, the midday sun fills my glasses with hot steam. Refocus. Refocus. Your patients are waiting. I pop open a bag of potato chips stashed in my handbag. Crunching the oily salt chips calms me. I wipe off my glasses with the corner of my damp white shirt. The lot across the street is filled with rubble, and the rats play shuffleboard with the rocks and the wind. It's a long way from my mother's pristine garden in suburban Massachusetts, I think, here, where I stand, on Valentine Avenue between 188th and 189th Street in the Bronx.

I straighten my bag on my shoulder, toss my head back, chew on my last potato chip and walk under a sun that laughs as it climbs slowly to the top of the sky. The open pump at the corner is filled with dancing children who, when they see me, nod and redirect the icy water's flow. "Gracias," I say and smile. I step off the curb and continue my journey. A U-Haul swings around the corner. Its thick wheels smack a puddle of water and bounce off the pavement, covering the cuffs of my navy- blue pants in mud.

The street holds its breath. I feel its eyes, and they are staring at me. I turn to look up 188th Street. The old men sit on their crates under a scrawny tree by Poe's Parking Garage. Their bags of beer are suspended in their hands, and the dominoes wait for the next move. The children cover their mouths, holding onto the sidewalk with one foot, or perhaps the other. A figure leans out of the alley and then quickly disappears.

"Damn," I say looking at the muddy cuffs of my pants. I lean over, gracefully, remembering my dancer days. I squeeze the water out of the cuff of my pants, smooth my clothing, rise and look around.

"Shit happens." And then I shake the sweat out of my hair, shrug my shoulders and laugh. The children catch my laughter, and I walk up the hill to the Grand Concourse.

A boy moonwalks through the cars, his boombox balanced on his shoulder. "Because I'm bad, I'm bad." He raises his chest and spins on the tops of his silver-tongued sneakers.

Strollers and bicycles weave in and out of the incessant movement of the crowd. Women undulate to the rhythmic poetry of the street. Young men flip cards in the corners of the alleys. The cars sneak around red, green and yellow lights, honking and hustling, cursing and carrying on, getting and going wherever it is that they are rushing to, or from. The smell of cigarettes, of hot dogs and beer, the sound of rap and horns and wheels, the taste of coquitos and mango emanate from the pavement that covers the rough, well-worn earth.

The hot asphalt is alive beneath my feet. I am grooving with my blue bag of bandages, swinging my hips inside my stiff navy- blue pants. Dancing, "cause I'm bad, I'm bad."

A figure walks towards me through the mirror of the Paradise Pawnshop. A thin, drawn, middle-aged white woman with dark granny glasses and stringy brown hair. She is dressed in navy-blue pants, a sweaty white shirt. A beeper is clipped to her belt. She is carrying an enormous blue bag of bandages that thrusts her forward with every step.

"Watch yourself, mommy," says a man who catches me before I walk into the window.

I pause before the reflection in the window. "Oh my," I say and continue on my way. "Can't be." I shake my head in disbelief. But still, I turn around to look once more at what is left behind. "But it is," and I recognize the image as my own.

It passes on, this life, outside of our control.

IN THE HOUSE OF MY FRIENDS

Deborah Williams-Camps

And one shall say unto him, What are these wounds in
thine hands? Then he shall answer, Those with which I
was wounded in the house of my friends.
Zechariah 13:6 (KJV)

My greatest life lessons will come to me by any means necessary. My most valued spiritual lesson occurred over a span of seven years, in a building located on Rev. James A. Polite Avenue off 163rd Street, from being hired as secretary to being FIRED as secretary. You're FIRED.... a term I've heard a few times throughout my career. All instances were unexpected, without warning, if you will. The angst of how am I going to pay rent, gas and electricity, car note, car insurance, food, keep my child in private school weighed heavy on my mind each time. My world was crashing in on me suddenly, notified and escorted out the door within an hour. Being fired as secretary was the most spiritually devastating in that if I had not been as rooted and grounded in the Carpenter, Jesus Christ, as I was I know I would've literally, lost my sense of right thinking, questioning my most valued relationship. ***WHO GETS FIRED AS CHURCH SECRETARY?*** How is this accomplished? How does one go about alienating the Senior Pastor to the point of no communication with myself at all? Have I entered the Twilight Zone? I surely missed the "do not attempt to adjust your set" warning. Yet it wasn't the Twilight Zone, it was the reality of my life. To sever ties with those I loved, considered family for over 30 years—without warning—was indeed cruel and inhuman treatment, no doubt about it. I attended this church with my dear grandmother Ma Dear as a youth.

It was a sunny warm day in August, I was in the church office when suddenly *Ms. Personnel and Deacon Personnel* entered. I was handed a letter signed by the Senior Pastor which stated I was fired effective immediately as my vision for the church office did not line up with his vision for the church office. Of course, the letter made no sense as we never had a conversation regarding the vision for the church office, ergo, how do we arrive at my being fired? **Disclaimer:** *Anything and everything the enemy does is not going to make sense, nor is it going to line up with GOD's Word, truth or integrity.*

Ms. Personnel and *Deacon Personnel* stood in my office and watched as I packed up five years of belongings, telling me what I could and could not take (not permitted to take my personal office logs nor was I allowed to obtain a copy). Needless to say as a writer this was salt ground into my wounds. My record of who called/visited office, why and the outcome, STOLEN. Mind you, those were two logs at most, the previous logs, seven years' worth, were at home (HUGE Smiley Face here). If I'd seen it coming, I would have taken home a copy of the office log daily. I was escorted to my car like a criminal.

Following this most mental, emotional and spiritually traumatizing event I sent certified mail letters to every Trustee and Deacon regarding my being fired, they were signed for by a church minister and never delivered to the persons the letters were addressed to. Then there was the incident of an associate Reverend stating she would not pray for me regarding my impending surgery. Following my recuperation there was a sit-down at my request, her reasoning for making the statement was because I would not tell her the circumstances for the surgery. **NONE OF YOUR BUSINESS!**

I know exactly why I was fired: I was not then, nor am I now, a pushover, YESSUM, kiss-ass personality. I followed the Word of GOD to the best of my ability regardless of the unethical, downright ungodly, going ons I was privy to. In my attempts to perfect the operations of the church office: My request for access to Food Pantry was denied on more than one occasion. Persons coming to the church in need of food were continually denied. I did not comply with the request NOT to spread the knowledge Jesus loved them to youth attending an alternative school within the church, often times seeing them escorted out of the school shackled ankles and wrists, headed to prison. I cried every time I witnessed this, some asked to see me before they were taken away. My only allegiance is to Jesus Christ, it was paramount they knew they were forgiven by GOD, they must forgive themselves, move forward on their life journey as best they could. Those students getting into trouble in the classroom would often be brought into my office so I could talk with them. My first statement, *always*: Who is your real enemy? Their answers varied (parents, teachers, those they did not get along with, etc.) not true, your truest, most authentic enemy: the devil, whose primary mission is to destroy you by any means necessary. They left our discussion with a spiritual perspective for their life journey and a hope for a brighter, positive future. My Bible says: Go out and make disciples. I even received a letter stating if I continued to witness to the alternative program youth I would be suspended and or fired as church secretary. I posted this letter on the wall of my office for all to see, as well as to remind me of this directive AND how it was not Biblical. Yes, I was not obedient to those who had 'rule' over me in this regard; the risk was worth GOD using me to have the eyes and ears of others opened to the wiles of the enemy in their life. There were many unbiblical practices and goings on within this particular branch of Zion, many of which I am quite sure I had no idea of. Granted, I was not prepared for most of what I witnessed and experienced in what was supposed to be my dream job. I was rudely awakened and I only knew how to stand on GOD's Word. In the beginning of my journey as church secretary I would go to the altar and pray on my knees, seeking God's face and by the time I was fired the spiritual toll was great, there was no love, no appreciation, no fairness, no do the right/ethical thing where I was concerned but rather constant blame, finger pointing, punishment, suspensions without pay, health insurance withheld for over a year, etc.

A member for over thirty years, church secretary for the last seven years…seven being the number of completion biblically speaking.

The Crux, the takeaway from this experience—I have learned never say never. I used to say I would never find myself out of the organized church. I loved GOD that much, I am a soldier for GOD. All has held true except for being in the organized church. I recently found a new church home, a vibrant, alive, community-oriented church where love is shown, where ALL, regardless of race, color, sexual orientation, are welcome. I soak up the teachings as a rock-hard sponge to water, *living water*. I am a survivor. I am still standing, stronger than ever, I've learned my most valued lesson to date: *I cannot expect to find my level of integrity or honesty in others, anywhere I may find myself including the organized church and this should not deter me in any way, shape or form from carrying out my God-given assignment for this life I have been blessed with.* **My only allegiance is to Jesus Christ.** Everyone and everything else is second. This in no way means I am perfect, none are. I strive for perfection, excellence, truthfulness and integrity in all of my dealings. When I find I have fallen short, when I have offended someone whether I agree with it or not, I must sincerely apologize to that person in that it is their perception which is their truth and I must make it right as my paramount relationship with Jesus Christ will ultimately be affected. I must seek forgiveness from others as I seek forgiveness from God.

Ten years later GOD and I still have a conversation on occasion; should I have stayed, stood my ground and been the spokesperson GOD wanted, needed me to be or should I have moved on, it was GOD's battle not mine. Perhaps GOD allowed me to see all I saw because He knew I had the backbone to stand against all that was not of Him on Holy Ground. The reason I did not remain as a member.… GOD hates six things, the seventh being an abomination to Him.

Proverbs 6:16-19 King James Version (KJV)

These six things doth the LORD *hate: yea, seven are an abomination unto him:*

A proud look, a lying tongue, and hands that shed innocent blood,

A heart that deviseth wicked imaginations, feet that be swift in running to mischief,

A false witness that speaketh lies, and **he that soweth discord among brethren.**

Statements I made in Bible study, etc. were misconstrued; taken the wrong way…. I thought it best to not be present in this branch of Zion any longer. I could not be seen or viewed as a sower of discord in God's eyes.

People always see JOY in me, receive encouragement from me never knowing the deep spiritual wounds I bear.

My truest bottom-line take away….do no harm, GOD's got me, I never stand alone, Jesus is right there with me. At this writing I am currently transitioning towards my Paradigm Shift: New Roads in my life journey. In hot pursuit of all the entities which bring my spirit joy and spread joy, hope and truth to others through my writing, photography and gift of exhortation, encouragement and counsel. I am determined to release all of my God-given potential into the waiting universe for the benefit of all mankind for generations to come. In JESUS name, Amen!

In everything give thanks: for this is the will of God in
Christ Jesus concerning you.
I Thessalonians 5:18

WHAT'S GOING DOWN IN THE BOOGIE DOWN?

Denessa Bachelor

The Bronx is considered to be the poorest county of
the state. The image comes with low expectations for family
life. However, I didn't think about that as I grew up. Now,
sometimes I do. The community seemed like a normal place
where people worked, lived and went to school. Not every
area looks like a congested city. Some parts look almost like
the countryside despite the stereotypical images that are
presented.

There are different kinds of families who reside here
whether their lineage in this county goes back generations or
they've been here a shorter time. I have relatives mostly in the
U.S., the Caribbean and England. Some of my family came
here from the Caribbean long before I was born to the rhythm
of this city. Like my family, many came here for different
reasons and may end up calling this place home.

Living in this neighborhood may not seem like it could
provide opportunities but it can and does for some. There are
people known to hold down more than one job. Others can
get by with just one. The worse would be not ever having
enough which can lead to all sorts of complications to get by.
That's part of the reason for robberies, petty theft and other
crimes. Businesses can thrive here but there have been
businesses in recent years that are no longer here. I remember
going to the American Theatre almost regularly before it closed
and Whitestone Multiplex Cinemas, like the American Theatre
have been around for ages only to make room for shopping
centers. More places are being demolished to build shopping
centers or affordable housing, only problem is everyone has a
different idea of what is affordable. These places were great for
friends and families to go and be entertained. Now residents

have to go farther to get a little excitement or find other options.

These other options especially for the young could pose a problem. Some kids will do anything if they think they can get away with it. My experiences growing up may not have been luxurious but it wasn't bad. I didn't cause my family real serious problems like being a teenage mother, abusing anyone or joining a gang. These are the descriptions I have been hearing about the Bronx or any area that isn't highly regarded. I dislike accusations about a whole community when someone doesn't know them. It might be true for some but saying all might be risky, but I guess they want to take the risk.

Life is what you make it around here. You can worry about what's coming next or keep things lit with your inner light. The dreamers, rebels and innovators are all here. Like it or not, here we are. This is what's going down in the boogie down.

NO MORE PASSING THE ZOO

Destiny Padilla

May of 2001, before 9/11 turned New York City into a grey desert, Queens was a shiny place with nice movie theatres and where the Chinese food tasted different. States Island was a place I'd never seen but teachers would talk about it and show us pictures of a huge boat that went there. Brooklyn was anyone who lived in the Bronx's arch nemesis. Manhattan was Manhattan. A shining jewel with skyscrapers and furniture stores that sold couches that weren't covered in plastic. The Bronx was home. A triangle of immigrant dreams that whispered, "grow up to be a doctor, teacher or lawyer". A car window and a six-year-old me played stay awake while Mom drove me and Sister to school every morning. On Wednesdays, the West Farms train staircase that looked like the staircases used to get on roller coasters would be filled with groups of families that resembled the families I gazed at on sitcoms. They always sported camping sized book bags, sandals and sunscreen that wasn't rubbed into their skin.

My elementary school was on Belmont Avenue and every year we would take the one trip the school budget could afford to walk to, the zoo. After school Abuela would pick me and Sister up and walk us to her house where Dad lived and Mom would come pick us up after work. Routine is to kid as routine is to the working adult, important. A Tuesday at Abuela's house waiting for Dad to bust through the door from work so we could do our running to Daddy routine show in front of any family that was over Abuela's house. Uniform dress itching my legs as nickelodeon watched me. Looking out of the window until the streetlights turned on and music got louder on the street. Dragging my feet to find Wela. He's taking forever today! Ta trabajando mija! Dropped myself on the corner of his bed until the sound of the door opening picked me up. Ran to the living room to do our usual Daddy got "home" from work ritual. The running stopped when I saw Daddy standing next to a woman I never met before. My eyes fixed on her bright red lipstick, her big white toothed smile and his arm being hooked onto her as he told me to say hello and give her a kiss. Back to the room. Sister was there. Daddy's here, with this lady. Mami told me and sister weeks earlier we may meet a new friend of Daddy's and when we did to tell her. Daddy hugged us before we went downstairs as usual. Don't tell your Mother you met Daddy's friend. I'll tell her, okay? Kiss. We got into the back of Mommy's black car. Left back seat, sister and me right back seat. How was schoolgirls? Good, good. What did Abuela make to eat? Chicken, rice. Oh sounds good girls. Stop sign. Sister. We met Daddy's friend. The car made a U turn. Back into the direction of the zoo. Going fast. No talking. Radio was turned off. Back at Wela's house. Stay in the car girls and whatever you do not come out! You hear me? Yes, yes. A chunk of eternity passed and Mom got back in the car. The cars passed the cracked window as we sped away from Abuela's house.

We passed the zoo, that's how I always knew we were almost home, we'd pass the zoo. The car window showed me routine. People walking with different movies on their eyes. This place is a cold weathered jungle, people, family, ripped visitor maps. Green gates that locked school trips each year. Hearing "the Bronx Zoo is the biggest metropolitan zoo in the United States" meant, world. Importance of home. This menial fact made life seem important. Lucky to be here in the Bronx with animals other than rats and roaches. Silverbacks, baboons, peacocks.

On this hazy ride back to West Farms I thought about the class bully Kaymon. How that year Teacher placed him in my group because Dad was the chaperone. She said he wouldn't mess with a big guy like my Dad. I remembered Kaymon's snack being a peanut butter jar, a plastic knife, and one white piece of sliced bread which he began preparing himself before Dad bought him chicken fingers and fries from the food court. I remembered Kaymon walking around the gift shop and stopping and staring at a squishable monkey head toy. I remembered Kaymon's tears cutting through the ashiness on his face like two zigzagging rivers. I remember Dad buying him the squishy monkey head and him chewing on it with his tear stained face. I remember how he didn't talk to me, ever. I remembered how my best friend Crystal was in our group too and said she wished her parents came on her trips to the zoo with her, how she felt like crying when we lined up to get into our trip groups but she didn't because crying was for babies. I thought about the smiling waving parents, me jumping up and down when I saw Dad, me holding onto his hand the entire trip.

Tomorrow showed up and school was out. Teacher told me I had to go to after school not regular dismissal where Abuela would be waiting with an icey or a bag of chips. I made new friends at after school. We did homework together and played board games. Sandwiches took the place of Abuela's island kitchen magic. Home isn't where you spend the most time. It should be. No Wela. No nickelodeon, no salsa blasting, no smells of Abuela's cooking, no waiting for Dad, no screaming at seeing the waterbug having wings.

No more passing the zoo.

JUST ME AND MY BABY: RAINY DAYS IN LITTLE ITALY

Lucy Aponte

A warm summer day in August of 1966. Inside our two-bedroom first floor apartment on Beaumont Avenue and 187 Street, the rhythmic splitter, splatter of raindrops bouncing off the windowpane of the nursery makes me melancholic. The skies are dark and gray. Five- month-old Kim sleeps peacefully, as I kiss the top of her head; burying my face in a full head of soft baby curls. Taking a whiff of the sweet baby scent, I think this day is a wash. We just moved in a few months before. I love taking my baby girl for walks and showing her off. Little Italy was a part of my childhood days. Going shopping to the Italian Market and making Artuso's Bakery a must stop for pastries and sweets was our weekly ritual on Saturdays. Shopping in Little Italy with Mama, my paternal grandmother who raised me in the Bronx was always a time of excitement. I knew we'd go to Artuso's Bakery for the soft, delectable almond cookies, the candied almonds with their delicate pastel blue, pink and yellow colors. I reveled in sucking off the color, then chewing the softened almond inside. I remember biting into soft little cream puffs and bringing my nose in to inhale the scent of sweet, baked goodness. The Italian festival in August isn't complete without a bag full of fresh, hot Zeppoles, smothered in powdered sugar inside the bag. Eating as you walk and licking powdered sugar off your lips is a part of the experience. You finish it all before you even get home. The Little Italy experience is a gastronomic delight.

Suddenly, the splitter splatter on the glass beckons with its rhythmic call. The scent of wet clean fresh air wafting up calls to me. This too is a moment for making memories. With the rain outside, the streets will be empty and quiet. A perfect time for just baby and me. I want my baby to be adventurous, curious, excited about life and to experience the wonders of the world just waiting for her out there. I want to make a connection with her. My mother didn't raise me, but I have strong memories of times I spent with her. As a motherless child, I missed out on many Mother/Daughter memories without her. I want more for my daughter. In the rain there will be nobody, or just a few people outside. The world will be for just me and my baby. I get excited for the new adventure. Quick as I can, I get dressed and get my little Kim ready for a rainy day walk in our Little Italy in the Bronx. All pretty in pink, I pick her up and lay her in the pram. She's just begun to sit up but cannot do so for too long. My baby has to see the world out there. Raising the recliner behind her in the pram she can enjoy the sights in comfort. The rain-cover over and across the pram will keep her dry from the rain, while the plastic face protector allows her to see the sites. I push the pram out into the narrow building hallway, lock the apartment door behind us and head out and down the steps to the sidewalk outside. I raise the hood cover, pushing the lock secure to keep her head dry. Then, I stick her little hand out and over the face protector so she can feel the rain drop splatters on her fingers. The rain will be her playmate as we walk. My baby will experience nature firsthand. The rain drops fall. Kim's eyes widen in surprise, as the liquid drops touch her skin. With each drop her eyes blink. She is in awe. Her fingers try to catch and hold onto the drops. She rolls her fingers around trying to capture the illusive raindrops. I am witness to a world through new-born eyes. Everything around her is new, everything is a marvel, a mystery, a wonder to explore. "That's the rain, baby," I whisper. "Feel the rain?" "It's wet and slippery." "Listen to the rhythm of the splitter, splatter." "The rain is talking, the rain is singing, the rain is dancing just for you." How exciting this is. Now, where will we go for a special treat, I wonder. At five months, Kim is too young for Artuso's Bakery and all the delicious pastries. That will be for later. I remember; just around the corner going east on 187th Street and Crotona Avenue is a pharmacy. Inside, the owner, Frank, has a baby book display case. I love books and so I enjoy reading to my baby. Walking slowly and purposefully, I inhale taking in the wet fresh air, thinking I want my baby to take in the experience as long as she can. Slowly, we turn the corner going east. As I walk, a slim young man with long blond hair and a bandana around his head looks at me. Approaching, the young man smiles. "Peace to you and your baby," he says, handing me a single daisy.

Surprised and touched, I whisper back, "And peace to you, as well." Like myself, he is a Flower Child. Touched and moved by the purity and beauty of the gesture, I carefully place the single daisy in the pram for my baby. This to me is an omen for the future of love, peace and understanding from the world to my child.

Continuing our walk, we get to the pharmacy. Opening the door, I push the pram inside.
We are engulfed in bright lights, as compared to the stark darkness of the rainy day outside. Shaking the rain off me, I say, "Hello," to the owner, unhook the rain cover, push down the lock to the hood to close it down and take Kim in my arms. "What are you doing out here in the rain," he asks. "My baby and I are getting a book to read today." "Oh," he marvels with a look of curiosity on his face. With Kim in my arms, I walk over to the display case. "I thought today is just perfect for getting a book from you," I say to Frank, as I peruse the books. "Look, Kim, so many books for you." Which one shall we get? Taking my time to savor the experience, I select one book, pushing back the urge to purchase more. This will be our special rainy-day activity from now on, I decide. There will be many more rainy days to celebrate together. Each one will be a special time with a special book to match. Paying for the book, I feel pride as Frank looks at my baby with a smile on his face. We chat a little on this quiet, rainy day. A little time spent with no other customers around. "Thank you, Frank," I say as I get ready to leave. "See you on our next rainy day walk when we come for a new book." Settling Kim into the pram I

pull the hood back up, placing the book and bag on her lap, cover up my baby, and place her hand out to play with her friend, the rain. Taking our time, I walk as Kim tries to catch the rain drops between her fingers. Back we go, turn the corner, go west on 187th Street, to Beaumont Avenue, turn left going north and slowly pull the pram into the building on Beaumont Avenue. "Say bye-bye rain," I quip. Inside we go, take off our clothes to settle in for a cozy story time moment. Just me and my baby, a book and a memory of a walk in the rain in my Little Italy in the Bronx. This becomes our rainy-day routine. A time to connect and to bond with my little girl. A special time for us on rainy days.

Reading books to my child has always been a special time to make Mother/Daughter memories. Thank you to the Flower Child for the daisy and to "Frank" the man at the pharmacy with the baby book display, on Crotona Avenue and 187 Street, and to
Little Italy in the Bronx for the memories. I will never forget the rainy days in Little Italy for just me and my baby.

THE WAY WE CRY

By Renee Bray

I have been silently suffering; I need to have a voice. I act as if I was the only one with depression and anxiety. When I admit I have it, I meet others who have, or had it. Even my therapist who treated me in the hospital had it. I become more human by sharing, and this disease—depression—becomes less vile and disgusting and becomes a biological reaction to pain and suffering. Thus, as I speak, I find my humanity and find others to be human. That's why I need to speak.

Mom will screech and say, "Why did you write this? Who cares if I did that? That's none of anyone's business." Dad will say, "That's not what happened, I wasn't that bad. I'm a great black father. That's how you took it. You should be over it anyway! Then you wouldn't have had to write about it! What's wrong with you?" My brother will say, "I did the best I could, you should have written about me. You know how Mom and Dad are. They drive you crazy." A classmate from my elementary school will say, "You did that to your best friend? What's wrong with you?!"

I won't write about or tell people how my parents didn't love me. I won't tell people how my paternal grandmother was a functional alcoholic, who survived a fall to her face, how she let strange people into her home. Or she survived constant late nights at the bar. I won't tell anyone how my dad said that you should be grateful, because no one else (parent) would put up with what you do. And I never was grateful, but I wanted to run away from home instead, but didn't. I won't tell people that I lived in the projects; it was too shameful and horrible especially in college when some fellow students were born in other countries. So, they probably wouldn't know what the projects are, or never even heard of those words), "The Projects."

I will tell the audience in advance that I have a brother eleven and half years old than me, but I'm not going to mention him. We didn't do much together, but then again I don't remember him so much. He moved out to live with my grandmother when he was nineteen and I was seven, then when he lost his apartment, he moved back. I remember he took me to the park on the weekends sometimes, but I believe he was often busy with school and his friends. We don't talk much now, he doesn't live in the city, and I would say we drifted apart, sort of estranged.

What I will write is how my family cries, particularly, the way my mother and I cry.

I never saw my dad cry. When he's sad, he just gets angry instead. I didn't even see him cry when my grandmother, his mother, died. I was twenty-one years old when she died. I tried not to cry in front of him because he didn't like crying. He often told me to stop crying as a little girl.

Only once I saw my mom cry. I was about five, or six years old. I came into the kitchen she was trying to open something with the back of a knife. It seemed like she hurt herself and she started to whimper. I ran over to her and saw her hand, it wasn't bleeding. I had sensed it was more than the bruise. She cringed, but not much tears came out. Finally, she stopped, and composed herself. She always had a stiff demeanor about her. She sort of whisked me out of the kitchen, saying she was fine softly, yet bluntly. To this day, I don't know what she was crying about for sure. I have a feeling she was missing her mother. My maternal grandmother died when I was about two or three years old.

Once I cried during a movie, and I was in the company of others, like a field trip. I was sobbing wailing in fact. Tears rolled down my eyes, repeatedly like a line of marching men. The movie scene was of a man on the floor of his room in a psych ward, digging in his arm with his nails looking to find an implanted device in his arm. A hospital staff comes in the room and reported to him his condition. The man finally comes to the realization that he hallucinated several events. This highly intelligent man discovered that he had schizophrenia. "A Beautiful Mind" was the movie.

I didn't leave the auditorium while I cried. No one told me to get up and cry in the bathroom. I was with a group of people who had their own mental health issues. We were clients of a Day Treatment Program, for people with mental health illnesses. The movie was picked so we could see how a man recovered from mental illness. It was a beautiful movie. I enjoyed it, but I wouldn't watch it again, once was enough for me.

EVOLUTION OF HIP HOP

Crystal D Mayo

The evolution of **Hip Hop** was like..... **GANGA.**

It rose from the crevices of concrete corners and scaled rickety stairs of tenement fire escapes with a pungent odor of the nitty gritty streets. It spoke in foreign tongue of rhythm and beat but its voice..... was ours, so we embraced it with a strange familiarity. Our translation was universal. It made our heads bob and fingers snap in unison. It made us congregate in huddles under lamp-lit basketball courts, waiting for that..........   **HIT**.......from fingertips that rolled its raw sound into bamboo leaves, lick the blunt with its greedy tongue then smoke us till it got ...**HIGH.**

The more it got lifted,

the more it grew......

Head

Arms

Limbs

Knotty dreads of a Rasta who puffed and passed us for his sustenance

Each puff sucked us deep down into his musical cavities that shook with base, then spit us out in thick smoke rings

Winding

Gyrating

In still air

Each puff gave birth to sound so potent

It shook teenage boys into convulsions

Then raised their bodies from the dead

Re-sculpting them into

Agile shapes suspended in mid-air

Then twist them into threads by the crowns of their heads

That one voice

Birthed infectious voices of

Griots rooted in jazz and rhythm

Telling urban stories through metaphorical blues

Carving similes out of syllables

Using lips and larynx as vocal percussion

And back then we didn't know

Over twenty-five years later

Strips of cardboard

Graffiti stricken trains

Adidas shell tops with fat colored laces

Suede Pumas

Lee jeans

Bamboo door knockers

Cazal glasses

Dookie rope chains and four finger rings

Would become **Hip Hop's** ancient artifacts

In the heat wave of 1984

East 152nd street became the Giant Rasta's personal dancehall

His train of knotty dreads

Swept the garbage from the street

Shook glass windowpanes with bass from his swollen feet

But on the 70th day of summer

He caught heat stroke

Collapsing with a sound of thunder

He was the **blackout** that caved in concrete

They say

Harlemites laid across his left arm in vigil

Chanting

Underground in the creases of his palm

Queens inscribed lyrics in his right hand

Authenticating his fist into a national monument

While his blood was still warm Brooklyn

Cut the skin from the sole of his left foot

Pressed it into shiny wax and sold thousands

They say the Rasta's left toe

Could be seen bobbing in the cold Staten Island water emerged

into the ingredients of the American Melting Pot

Mount Vernon oiled his coiled dreads

Till they crowned his head like a lion's mane

180th street in the Bronx ceremoniously closed his eyes

Kissed his swollen cheeks then tenderly traced his lips

Chapped from the cut and scratch of his last syllables

Gunhill Road climbed his shoulders like Mt. Everest

Spitting impromptu uncensored lyrics across his collarbone

But his heart

His heart belonged to us

The South Bronx

East 152nd Street

With diligent hands

We crushed open lime and sand

For his burial ground then thousands of solicitous hands

Carried his warm arteries to the handball courts in the big park

Is final resting place

The wall was his headstone

His epitaph carved in flamboyant letters with indelible ink

And when all was buried beneath

Not one of us shed a tear

See **Hip-Hop** hadn't died

Its heart pulsated on as we made it our own

Every time brothas and sistas freestyled on the block

Or the cut and scratch of the needle found its spiral groove, it

was proof that we had internalized it would spread into

A world epidemic

And over time it transitioned

Transforming into other life forms

The music of our indigenous culture

Spread into an epidemic

Hip Hop

Was the soundtrack to my adolescent life

A medley of archives for my coming of age stories

The chronicles of a little girl

Growing into herself through Collages of

Lyric and life's still pictures

Pasted on Harmonious pages

The Evolution of Hip Hop

Was the Evolution of Me

MY NEW HOME

Ron Trenkler-Thomson

I became a Bronxite in the mid-1990s, when I rented a small room in a two-bedroom apartment on the first floor of a six-story building on Allerton Avenue and Bronx Park East. From the two small windows of my room I could see cars and pedestrians and, across the street, Bronx Park. My "landlady" was a widow, a wonderful woman in her 70s who liked to socialize and cook for me. I was very happy living there.

But after four years, having reached my mid-20s, I decided it was time that I got my own apartment. I now held a full-time job and could afford to rent one. The thought of uprooting myself dismayed me, though. Move all my belongings again? Start anew somewhere else, where I'd have to meet new neighbors? Make new friends? Thoughts that others might have found exciting frightened me.

Screwing up my courage, I went to a real-estate office in the neighborhood. I knew that I wanted to remain in the Bronx. I had gotten used to this borough and liked the diversity of the people, the abundant places to shop, and the many green spaces and parks. The broker who introduced herself to me seemed quite optimistic about finding an apartment for me that I would like.

First she showed me two one-bedroom places, each in a pre-war, red-brick building. Both looked nice, but picky me— who wanted bright light and not shade—had problems with each. One had a tree right in front of the living room windows, which meant the sun hardly had a chance to shine in. The second apartment looked over a backyard with buildings on each side and no view of trees or other growing things.

As we left the second place, I pointed to a high-rise post-war building across the street, remarking how modern it looked with its beige bricks and large windows. The broker turned to me and said, "Oh, do you like those kinds of buildings?" I nodded. So she said she would drive me to another part of the Bronx, where she knew of a vacant apartment in such a building.

We drove west, past the Bronx Zoo and Botanical Garden. We crossed Grand Concourse and Sedgwick Avenue and then drove over the Major Deegan Expressway. I had never before ventured that far west.

We arrived in a neighborhood known as Kingsbridge and stopped at a 15-story building on Broadway. With the super, we took the elevator to the eighth floor, where he led us to a vacant studio apartment. I had never lived in a studio and had hoped to find a one-bedroom. But this apartment blew me away. The combined living room/bedroom was large enough to fit a sofa bed, table, and other furniture. The separate kitchen had large cabinets and plenty of storage space. There was a large closet in the living room and another in the hallway near the bathroom. When I looked through the large windows and saw the beautiful unobstructed view across Broadway all the way to Bailey Avenue, as well as the balcony attached to the living room, it was love at first sight. Moreover, the nearest subway station was only a few blocks away, so commuting to my job in Manhattan would take less time than from my Allerton Avenue room. And adding extra sweetness to the deal, the studio was rent-stabilized!

I immediately exclaimed to the broker, "I'll take it! Where do I sign?" She explained that first I would have to fill out an application so that the management company could run background checks and determine whether I was qualified to become a tenant in the building. Fortunately, it all worked out, and I was able to move in a few weeks later. Little did I know that this would be my home for the next 15 years.

It didn't take long to get to know people in my new building. In the first week after my move, a woman from my floor, curious to meet her new neighbor, introduced herself. "Hi, I'm Debra. Welcome to our floor!"

Debra became a very good friend: we shared our histories and family experiences, and spent time together. I saw her son growing up. A few times when they traveled out of town on vacation, I stopped by every day to feed their cat and take care of the litter box.

Soon I met the other neighbors on my floor and a few from other floors as well. We united and complained to management when there was no hot water or heat in the winter in our apartments. And we joined to face bad neighbors who made our lives hell.

One day I saw a flyer advertising a small fitness studio that had opened on the first floor of the building. I had never dared going to a gym, but I knew that I badly needed to start working out to improve my health. That is how I made another friend—Juan, who had started the fitness business with a partner and who worked as a personal trainer. I came for my first appointment a few days after meeting him. I remember on that first day, Juan suggested that I warm up on the treadmill. I lied when he asked, "Have you been on a treadmill before?" But when he noticed my confusion, he showed me how it operated.

I continued working out at Juan's gym for two years, until he moved on to start other enterprises. Though he's no longer my personal trainer, we remained good friends. I saw his daughters grow up, and his family and I even vacationed together.

While living on Broadway, I also joined a writers' group that meets in the Kingsbridge branch of the New York Public Library once a week. Writing proved to be an excellent outlet for me, and it became a rewarding avocational activity. I also made new friends there.

Unfortunately, after a few years I began to have problems in the building. The studio next to mine was like a revolving door, with a steady stream of different tenants. One year, a pregnant single mother moved in with her two young children. The toddler seemed to cry nonstop, day and night, while the older boy played with his ball, throwing it against the wall that my apartment shared with theirs. When I knocked on their door and asked the mother whether I could help her or with her children in any way, she turned me down and asked me to leave her alone.

After she left, a young man moved in—quite the party person! Loud music blared and guests trooped in and out way past midnight, even on weekdays. When I complained to him, he insisted that he had the right to do whatever he wanted to within his own four walls. The manager of the building refused to do anything about that situation, and the landlord wouldn't help either. They also did nothing about the noisy couple who lived on the floor above mine, even though several other neighbors joined me in alerting them to the deafening music they played into the wee hours of the night.

My sleepless nights began to take a big toll. Reluctantly, I made up my mind to leave the apartment that had served as my home for over a decade.

A few years ago I moved into a building in a nearby neighborhood. However, I still enjoy the weekly writing circle at the Kingsbridge library. I also began attending open-mic evenings in Kingsbridge and elsewhere.

I sometimes wonder how different my life would be if I hadn't left the building on Allerton Avenue and formed good friendships along the way in a different section of the Bronx. I'm glad I took the risk of moving, not once but twice. The fears I harbored of starting anew in different neighborhoods proved to be groundless. And I'm also glad that I remained in the Bronx. I can't imagine living anywhere else!

A DAY I WON'T FORGET

Anneros Valensi

I loved my store in Riverdale in the Bronx. Not far from my home, for five years, I owned a small boutique in which I sold clothes and gifts geared toward women, children, and babies. Women as well as men came to my store to browse and buy merchandise, which I changed seasonally. I also sold holiday items. Men bought gifts for their girlfriends or wives. Even high school students came to buy gifts for their friends. They stopped by after school. My own children at that time were in middle school.

During the first year, nothing out of the ordinary happened in my store. I was aware of no robberies in other stores on the street, but I did read in newspapers about occasional crimes in our neighborhood.

One day in the second year, two guys walked into the store. Most of my customers were regulars, and I had never seen those two before. One was a short, pretty ordinary looking man, wearing regular pants and a shirt and no jacket. The other's attire was fancier: he wore a black suit, white shirt and fashionable tie. And he was very slim and tall.

The tall man seemed very curious. He started checking out the merchandise. He looked through the hangers as if determined to see everything: the blouses, sweaters, pants, skirts—every item. What seemed quite strange was the behavior of his companion. He had stopped at the entrance door as if guarding it. His back leaned against the doorway, preventing any prospective new customer from entering.

To me that looked very suspicious. It reminded me of a movie I once saw in which two guys entered a store. They both looked something like these two characters, especially the one standing as if to "guard" the store. Both their behaviors frightened me.

I asked the man close to me, "May I help you? Are you looking for something in particular?"

He looked at me, said nothing, and then turned away and kept browsing. His fancy clothing looked nothing like the outfits my regular customers wore. Nor do I remember anyone dressed that way in Riverdale walking on the streets. They dressed differently from my neighborhood people's regular or even fancy outfits I saw on weekdays or weekends. They dressed to be noticed.

They and I were the only ones in my store. I had no employees, and during that time in the 1980s few shopkeepers owned security cameras. I also didn't have pepper spray. The two men continued what they were doing, while neither one appeared to want to buy anything. I got restless and uneasy and started to wonder what would happen if another customer should want to come in. It didn't occur to me to imagine what would happen if one or both of them were to drag me into the back area next to the dressing room.

I started to think about what to do should they decide to grab hangers full of clothes and run out or collide with a customer coming in. I was so afraid, I remained standing tensely in the back, behind the counter, glancing at the cash register every few second. I didn't dare to pick up the phone to call the police while the men were still there. The whole situation seemed frighteningly spooky to me.

How can I get the attention of a police car, I wondered. I really hoped that a whole group of people would come in at once. It was nerve-wracking. I concentrated on the tall guy, watching all his movements. What did this silent browser want? Why was his companion still at the door? My eyes then scanned the street for a police car and to see if anything unusual was happening outside. Nothing out of the ordinary. I was left on my own.

Eventually, the tall man took a pair of earrings from the jewelry case and asked me to hold them until the next day. "We will come tomorrow to pick them up," he said. He sent a few more glances through the store and then they both left.

I was so relieved. The first thing I did was to call the police precinct expressing my discomfort. Though nothing was taken from my store, the officer was very kind and understanding about my situation. She made me feel more at ease, promising that police cars would patrol the neighborhood more frequently.

The next day I felt nervous as I opened my store. I kept looking left and right several times checking the street as I unlocked the door and walked in. Unlike on previous days, all day long I felt uncomfortable. Every time I heard the door open, I looked up immediately to see who it was and felt relieved when it was one of my regular customers. Two police officers visited me in the afternoon, asking whether everything was okay and if the two men had returned. "No, officer, they did not come back today," I said. One jotted down some notes on an official form, and then they left.

I saw police officers patrolling our shopping area more often thereafter. Fortunately, during the few years that I continued to maintain the store, nothing else unusual happened. I never saw the two men again. But I will never forget them.

OFF JACKSON AVENUE IN THE BRONX

Robert Gibbons

It was off Jackson Avenue, five years ago. I rushed down into a pit after leaving some of my possessions on a seat. The world went underground. The world I thought I knew, not a divided one, not a world that collided with this impossibility. My attention may have been drawn to art of Kandinsky or the constant graffiti that is in my head. They always overcrowd me in this crowded church. The anti-Semite or Nazi sympathizer, the late-night cruiser, even if you are a dancer, perchance you may chant to the wall, or fall down from intoxication. It was 86th, five years ago, near Lex, where I dropped a small male purse full of cash and credit cards, and I said, "Oh my God." I am done. This is New York. You just do not do this here in this city of petty cash. I punished myself with anxiety. I cried immaturely and sober. If I was drunk maybe I would have been more careful; when this city is so full of labels. In the back of my head I knew it would never return. I had been burned. Said to myself it was the late-night straphanger. They would cross it, look inside, toss it, and I would be dead upon arrival.

Said they would open my privacy, for now I would distrust the government, would still believe in a failed humanity. Would I believe in this long process of renewal, but for now, my wallet was missing. It was like searching for missing jewels. The drone behind glass would have no compassion. It was story that had been heard year after year; midnight after midnight. It was not sensational or romantic enough, it was too jade or downright trite. A sort of harassing voice answered, "Dropped your wallet sir, ha!" Would have preferred to say, "I would like to update my card or ask for proper direction, but, no." I dropped my wallet. I know there is a combination of protocols, a nursery of questions or even laughter about it behind the feign sophistication. "Sir, you dropped your wallet." Just call it taken, she thought and would not say. It was night but to her it was a daylight revelation.

Call it a shake down. Call it missing like the three thousand children living in the subway systems in D.C. or Chicago, or Detroit or Miami. This is a big system. There is a rhythm by which we do things. My wallet was one of them; a toddler, like the Romanian women that held her baby that night and asked for money. My wallet, I would fold her, place in a particular idea of order every day. If she were female, then she would be Bridget. If male, then he would be Charlie. What a way to end the day. The grief is in every step, each chance encounter. "Sir are you listening, your wallet is missing. If you dare to believe there is a lost and found on 34th but this is a sequence of fact." This is Jackson Avenue and not 34th Street; stop and frisk me right here.

"Tell them you dropped your wallet and they will take you through the process." It will take three years to go through grief and loss counseling. Another additional to receive the assurance there is not an inkling of identity theft. Tell them you are American, or Armenian. Tell them you are Jewish or Hebrew, sir, do you understand that you are missing in this city. You are invisible on an island of eight millions. You are nobody to me. Cop a plea, tell them you smoked marijuana two years ago and then your record will be sealed. Appeal to the counsel and maybe one day you will have a good government job.

It was the third rail. It was the smell of the old and the new, the consignment and the few that would be so lucky, that would be giving. So I did it. I made an appointment to the lost and found. Most people probably would give up. Some people bank on that. But this is New York, you can't. In my only hope, I began to gloat and smirk, beneath the limestone and sheet rock, beneath this steel clock. It was old and rusty. My insanity would not protect me. No wonder there are cables when the world is so unstable. I stood there beneath Frida Kahlo, beneath Gustav Klimt like the darkness of a Courbet painting; just waiting for my baby to return. I had earned the right to ask for her back. Among one thousand bags and socks, umbrellas, manila-colored pieces of history left in one room. Left like a doomsday of a subway tomb my baby returned. "Sir let me check," the fatal voice countered. Let me make sure you are pure. "Sir, you are fortunate, someone returned it, with cash, and card, attached with a note that said, "I found this off Jackson Avenue."

TEN THINGS I KNOW ABOUT THE EVENING I WAS BORN

Sydney Valerio

1. It was Sangibin which is the Dominican holiday for the third Thursday in November

2. Mami's due date was for the second week of December

3. My oldest aunt was hosting her siblings which meant that the men had to bring a box of beers & the women had to prepare a dish for the potluck

4. It had been only two years since the family moved from Harlem to the Bronx, rents were getting too high to be paid with a seamstress's wage, and the new apartment was a downsized version of the previous four bedroom

5. My father had hooked up with one of his side chicks the night before and the day started with an argument about why he had not come home

6. Your aunt had an ice filled washing machine stacked with four packs of Lowinbrowns by 3 p.m.

7. I think the dancing and eating before 5 is what made mami become dizzy or it could have been the woman standing outside your aunt's window looking for your father

8. The apartment already had a dozen people in it and windows had to be opened

9. The vinyl records on deck were of Fernando Villalona & La Gran Manzana

10. Mami wasn't ready for the way your body took all of the oxygen from hers

GRAND MOTHER ABUELA LAURA

George Colon

60 years ago, September 18, 1958, my saintly grandmother Laura Casado (born 1902) left us.

And this now retired teacher still sees his first teacher teaching him. Grandmother *Abuela* Laura holds a pencil in her hand—and in it, letters, her greatest legacy, yes, the magic of writing. In our South Bronx apartment after migrating again, she sits me down in our kitchen table next to the fire escape window. She teaches me, the little boy, to write letters. *"Mira, coge este lapis y ponga me las letras.* Take this pencil and put these letters on this paper." Her grandson—me—puts a pencil very early in his hand; I put its point to paper. *Abuela* writes the letters; I reproduce them. Yes, I would be a writer. Yes, I would be a teacher. Her compassion followed me into the classroom. Copied her lesson with my daughter and my grandchildren

Her spirit yet hovers over me.

My grandmother *Abuela* Laura lives in my memory and heart, a lovely, dark woman, always smiling, with black hair straightened with the electric iron comb of those days, her large black eyes filled with purpose and determination. She holds a bible in most photos. She raised and fed ten children during the Great Depression of 1930's when the U.S. sneezed, and Puerto Rico caught a cold. Uprooting herself, she moved with my grandfather from Puerto Rico's *Campo*, or countryside, to that shantytown on the outskirts of San Juan, before that propeller Plane to Hell's Kitchen, then the South Bronx. She babysat me, my sister and the many cousins that passed through our apartment while my mother and her sisters worked at the factory.

Abuela Laura grew ill and spent more and more time in the old Lincoln Hospital on 143rd Street and Southern Boulevard. Having ten kids and uprooting oneself takes its toll, especially during depressions. By the time the doctors diagnosed her renal disorders, her kidneys were shot. When I came home from school September 18, 1958, a Thursday, Mami gave me the news. "Abuela died." I didn't totally comprehend the full implication of death then. She wore a magnificent gown in her casket at the Ortiz Funeral Home on Prospect Avenue, near East 149th Street. I still smell the flowers over fifty years later and to this day associate them with death, not life.

Abuela read the bible, and though she baptized all her children Catholic, turned to the Pentecostals, though from time to time went to a catholic church. "I will enter wherever the Lord is present." Religion played an important role in Abuela's life—and mine. She worshiped in a Pentecostal storefront church on Longwood Avenue and once a week I accompanied her and those shouts, admonitions, and cries. "Hallelujah! Gloria A Dios! Hosanna's." But she did raise her children Catholic.

She treated Jewish and black neighbors courteously and they reciprocated her kindnesses. We all got along well at first. "*Quien quiere café?*" She always asked when neighbors and family called. "Who wants coffee?" She'd intervene on behalf of neighbors, broke up fights and settled arguments, always waving her bible. Abuela Laura's compassion hovers over me yet along with her spirit. Compassion and understanding. She did hit me a few times, for my own good, straightening this crooked oak who grew straight.

We said a rosary every night for a few nights before and after her burial, led by a fat lady dressed in white, in front of an old sewing machine also draped in white as makeshift altar. All our extended family showed up—the last time they all gathered. Her sisters Tia Lola, Tia Maria and cousins. Most of her children, including my aunt, Titi Isabel, who came from Puerto Rico feeling a premonition. Nieces and nephews and their kids. And some past borders, including Esmeralda, now married, having moved away. Hot chocolate was served.

Atop the makeshift altar, candles burn next to Lazarus' likeness, halo around his head, crutches in the hand, not yet dead, not yet brought back to life by Jesus, dogs at his side licking the saint's wounds. Jesus pictures and that of his mother adorn the wall. The fat lady chants and works the rosary beads. The candles' flames bend, nudged by a sudden breeze that moves the curtain. But they glow defiantly, hypnotizing me. *"Que Dios la saque de pena,"* the fat woman recites. "May God take her from her pain..."

"...*Y la lleve a descansar.* And take her to her rest," came the chorus.

A scream interrupted this monotonous drone one night. It was Esmeralda. Abuela Laura became like a mother to Esmeralda. My aunt Titi Julia cried, as did the fat woman. My grandmother's spirit entered. *"Quien quiere café?"* the spirit said. "Who wants coffee?"

No, I didn't see it, too busy cuddled by the breeze and hypnotized by the candle.

I didn't go to St. Raymond's Cemetery. My mother and Aunt Julia still visit the tomb. I sometimes drive them.

Her presence haunted me for years and she appeared in my dreams for a while. In them, she shows up at the house and at first, I thought nothing of it, but then think, "Wait aren't you dead?" Fearing this spirit, I bundled myself up in bed, even in hot weather. I fear the dead and death itself and always see them in sleep after wakes at Ortiz Funeral Home. Was it about the few times I stole pennies from her purse? Or maybe a lingering guilt about the time I accidentally pinched her finger on the bathroom door? Somebody tells me touching the dead cures one's fear. I tried it on Willie Carrasquillo from the block, who drowned in the East River. His cold hand lingers on my senses for a while. Only when my cousin Doris died years later would my fear end.

Mami says Abuela's spirit woke her up one night. *"El nene se esta ahogando,"* the spirit says. "The baby's suffocating." Mami rushes to my room and finds me covered in bed sheets, gasping for air. Mami goes through hard times.

After Abuela's death things get hard even though some of the boarders did double time as part time babysitters, as did my cousins. Mami prays to Abuela and asks for help.

"La *renta* is due and I'm short. Que si Con Edison. Que si winter is coming and I need a new coat. Que si pa'qui, que si pa'alla." And those men, they keep going AWOL.

One night, Abuela appears in the form of a skeleton.

"I'm dead, can't you see? I want to rest. You must solve your own problems from now on."

So, yes, Mami solved her own problems.

And a lot of mine.

"Mami, I've fucked up again. Can you lay some bread on me? Pay you next pay day."

Toma!" Here! *Amara te bien la correa.* Tighten your belt. Women. Money. Those friends. All that partying. Que si pa'qui, que si pa'alla."

And Abuela Laura? She bumps me on the head from heaven.

Yes, still feel her spirit and compassion hover over me and guide me yet.

MADE OF THESE

Joe Carrión

The building on Ryer Avenue was divided into two sections joined by a large lobby with a mirrored wall and a faux fireplace, the remnants of a former elegance. My grandmother lived in a single bedroom on the fourth floor that faced the avenue, and I moved there after my mother had finally run away from my evil stepfather Papo. This happened toward the end of my freshman year at Bronx Science. My little brother Adam had friends on Sedgwick near University Avenue, and so would often visit and walk back from there to my grandmother's apartment, which was just off 181 Street. When my sophomore year began in 1986, I was sleeping on a folding couch in between my aunt Ada and my aunt Josie, who was deaf and partially mute. I would do my homework listening to the small radio in the kitchen at night when everyone else was in bed.

After that first year in high school I felt out of my element because there were few students that I could relate to at "Science." I disliked two of my teachers and had gone from being the smartest student in the class in junior high, to just average at this school. My alienation would soon turn to indifference as I began getting high with my friends on the Grand Concourse. My sophomore year was supposed to be the time when students were to give serious consideration to studying for the SAT and preparing their college applications, but what I felt was contempt for all things academic. I had begun to use marijuana during the summer, and this continued throughout my time in high school.

One Saturday in November, I was returning from Shipman's hobby store on the Concourse with my childhood friend Albert, who I'd had known since I was 10 years old. It was late afternoon and I needed to get back to my grandmother's house to see my mother, who'd been there for the weekend. She was getting married once again and the wedding was to take place one week from then. Adam, Albert and I were going to be groomsmen in it and we had to rehearse. My brother had gone to our old neighborhood on Sedgwick Avenue and was late getting back. Albert and I ran up the four flights of steps of my grandmother's building anxious about what we were going to do that weekend. Bounding up the worn marble steps, I could tell what level I was on by the different foods I smelled as I passed each floor: Fried chicken on the 2nd floor, *arroz con gandules* on the 3rd floor. Once I reached the 4th floor, the smell changed to that of cigarettes and stale urine, maybe because the rooftop was one flight up. When my grandmother cooked that was the only time the 4th floor hallway didn't smell nasty. I'd always considered my grandmother a rugged type of woman, maybe because I never heard of anyone else say they'd seen their grandmother in a street fight, but I had—twice. She made good use of her hands when she created a dish too. Everything was ripped, smashed or shredded by hand. I'd sit at the kitchen table and watch her methodically smash the onions garlic, cilantro, peppers and salt in a mortal and pistil. The scent of the ingredients was a preview of the wonderful meal that would soon take shape. I often wondered how she knew what to add without tasting it. Only after everything was added and she prepared to cover it with the aluminum lid did she bring the big spoon to her lips and sip. My mother was never a good cook, but I forgave her for it because she was beautiful and carefree in a way that I found special, but sometimes held against her. She was not strict and I was never asked where I was going by my mother. Now, she seemed happy for the first time in years, and her wedding to her boyfriend Wilson after just a few months of dating was going to be celebrated with a trip to Cancun for her honeymoon.

Out of breath, I put my key into the tumbler that turned the old police lock. It usually didn't open up right away and I had to jiggle the key to get the pins to align themselves.

At the very moment when I felt the tumbler spin, the lock suddenly gave way and the door opened, leaving my keys dangling. My mother stood in the doorway and I could see she'd been crying. I didn't have a chance to ask what was wrong. "They shot him Joey! They shot him in the head!" She cried out. I didn't understand what she meant. Adam? It was a question, but it was also a response to what she had just told me. I felt my friend Albert's arm on my shoulder as my mother continued sobbing, telling me that Adam was in Jacobi hospital in critical condition. He was alive! There was relief when I heard this, but as the details unfolded, I understood that my brother would not be the same after this. Nothing would be the same afterward. That evening, my family waited to be allowed into the intensive care unit. When we walked in, his head seemed huge to me, and was completely wrapped in bandages. His eyes were closed and there was a strange expression—something between a smile and a smirk—on his face. The doctors said the swelling was caused by the large exit wound that shattered the cranial bones on the right side of his head; the trajectory of the bullet going through the occipital lobe and exiting just above his right ear. I looked at my mother, her eyes puffy and red from crying, and at my aunt Ada holding one hand to her mouth as her eyes reddened. I looked at Adam but didn't cry. Even my father was there, talking to the doctors. He angrily looked in the direction of my mother while he asked the physicians if Adam would ever be the same again. He blamed her, of course.

No one asked how I felt, and I left the hospital that evening feeling withdrawn and isolated. My mother was busy cancelling the wedding plans and informing the rest of our relatives of the tragedy. I cried in the shower that evening and thought about my little brother and the bullet entering his brain while he played a video game in that candy store on Kingsbridge road. Around the corner, in the grocery store, the owner said he had been cleaning his .44 caliber handgun and that it had accidentally discharged. If it hadn't been for the police that transported my brother to Jacobi hospital for fear that he would die before the ambulance got there, I don't think he would have survived. Adam had been wearing my leather jacket, which I eventually got back blood stained and sealed in a plastic bag. It had been cut in half to quickly remove it at the hospital.

As the days wore on I visited my brother less often, and when I did go I was high on marijuana. I cut school and spent more time hanging out on the Grand Concourse with my friends. I was 17, and I was smoking weed laced with crack cocaine. My friends Rob and Chino were always looking to get high and exploring other ways to escape reality. We were hanging out in the basement of a building on Creston Avenue that served as a drug spot one cold night in January when I saw Rob pull out a piece of aluminum foil and pass it to Chino. What were they sniffing? Chino passed the foil to me and I looked down at the beige powder. I couldn't tell by looking whether it was coke or heroin, and I knew that heroin wasn't what I wanted to try. Rob said it was coke, but I didn't trust him. He was always telling me I should try dope, and that it was incredible for having sex. I handed the foil back to rob, "I don't get down with p-funk," I told him. There wasn't going to be any negotiating on that. Instead, I walked over to the sofa where a young woman was waiting for me. I remember that her hair was up in two ponytails: one on either side of her head. I stood over her, surveying her delicate features as I tried to guess her age—17? 18? Rob handed her the tin foil as she looked up and smiled innocently at me. The pen cap used for sniffing had become oily from use, and she wiped it on her t-shirt while walking to the bathroom. I watched as she took two hits from the foil, turn the faucet on, and then held her wet hands to drip water into her nose. She walked back to the sofa and sat directly in line with my crotch and felt me through my jeans. There wasn't any small talk to speak of....

That night I walked through the freezing winter night carefully making my way on the icy surfaces of the sidewalk towards the subway. When I got to the top of the staircase, I could already hear the rumble of the train coming in from

Fordham Rd., and I hurdled over the turnstile and ran down the stairs as fast as I can. I jumped right in through the open D-train doors and quickly sat down on the southbound train. My heart was beating fast in my chest as I leaned my head back onto the aluminum panels and closed my eyes.

IS IT POSSIBLE TO DISLIKE SOMETHING YOU'VE LOVED FOR A LIFETIME?

Ted Mieszczanski

Yes, most definitely. I avoid some things because they carry me back to a reality that is no longer mine.

I don't go to the gyms or the playgrounds that once took up all my heart's time. It's too painful because that part of my life is over. Time has taken care of that.

But I do remember the one time I bought my son a new Spalding basketball as a gift. He kept reminding me that he'd never had a new ball, that he'd only gotten hand-me-downs. I knew I should have told him that I'd pay for it and that he should go with his mother. But he insisted he wanted to go get it with only me. Maybe it had something to do with all those times when he was little and watched me from the sidelines.

He certainly didn't need me. He was good, really good, in fact, better than I ever was. So I weakened and we went.

As soon as we entered Modell's on Fordham Road, I could smell the scent of new leather. But when my son placed the ball he wanted in my hand, a host of memories exploded right through my fingertips, racing along the elongated pathways of my nerves, leaping across synapses, going straight on to my brain.

And then I remembered everything that I'd sworn off.

I'm in the park on Bailey Avenue. It's a warm day and the air is sweet and fresh. The tall trees offer some shade from above, but it doesn't really matter. All I experience is the rock fitting in the upside-down cradle created by my palm and fingertips. I feel the vibrating rhythm of leather pounding on concrete, first speeding up, then slowing down as my body

121

changes directions right to left, shifting from one speed to another, keeping my backpedaling shadow off balance.

And finally, there's the struggle of bodies colliding in air as one tries to dominate the other, rising, always rising...

I taste victory and it is sweet. I taste defeat, strangely bittersweet.

I must let it all go. It all becomes too much to bear. The sting of what is gone has replaced the pleasure of reminiscing.

And now this new ball reminds me of what I can no longer have. Is that fair?

Of course, it is, why not! Nothing is promised.

But, isn't it strange that all this should be returned to me from only the scent of a new basketball sitting quietly on my fingertips, waiting, just waiting.

MY AVIAN VISITORS

Miriam Levine Helbok

The Bronx, with coordinates 40°50'14"N, 75°53'10"W, lies comfortably within Earth's northern temperate zone, but the borough is also home to such residents of the Arctic as polar bears and snow leopards, such tropical beasts as Malayan tapirs and white-cheeked gibbons, and such denizens of Antarctica as Magellanic penguins and Inca terns. Those animals do not wander at will about the Bronx, of course; rather, they live in captivity in the Bronx Zoo. The Bronx does provide room and board for some wild creatures, however, among them pigeons, sparrows, starlings, crows, bats, rats, mice; occasional raccoons, coyotes, rabbits, and skunks; and many squirrels. Squirrels scampering boldly about their business in the zoo made a far greater impression on a visitor from overseas whom I led on a tour of the zoo than any of the exotic animals on exhibit, because, she told me, she never saw a squirrel in her native city, Montevideo, Uruguay. To her, squirrels seemed remarkable, and freely roaming squirrels, incredible.

For six years, starting in the mid-1980s, I worked at the zoo, the barks of sea lions having provided a cacophonous accompaniment during my interview for the job. My office was in a small building behind the outdoor cages of some birds of prey, meat-eating birds also known as raptors: eagles, condors, and owls. I never expected to see any birds of prey up close and personal anywhere else, but two individuals from two raptor species have honored me briefly with their presence where I live, just inches from my face.

The first arrived several years ago on a day in winter warm enough for me to open the door to my 15th-floor terrace so that my cats could venture out. I was in the living room when I noticed Annie, my female cat, trot back inside. (The male had remained indoors.) To my astonishment, I saw a pair of feet, each with three large toes ending in extremely long, sharp talons, clutching the windowsill that sticks out into the terrace. Reptile-like scales covered the toes, but in my memory I have covered them with long hair, so that I immediately thought they belonged to some extraordinary mammal. The rest of the animal remained hidden from view. With my heart pounding I sprang to close the terrace door—and saw not a mammal but a huge bird. It was a red-tailed hawk, which was now upright, standing about two feet tall. I recognized it instantly because I had read Marie Winn's book *Red-Tails in Love—A Wildlife Drama in Central Park*, about a mated pair of red-tailed hawks that had made a nest on a ledge protruding from a high window of a building overlooking Central Park's model-boat pond. I had also watched a documentary about the pair.

As I gazed in wonder, the hawk stared at me looking out at it through the glass of the door. I will never forget its beauty and regal solemnity and the nobleness of its head, and especially its brilliant dark eyes. Then the bird turned and leaped to the front of the terrace, hooking its talons on the screen a few feet above the floor, so that it now faced east.

How could such a large bird have gotten into a fully screened terrace? Plainly, it had flown right through the screen at high speed. At the north end of the terrace, I saw a hole shaped somewhat like a scarecrow, the "head" a circular opening about the size of a softball, with rips a few inches long protruding horizontally from each side of the circle where ears might have been, and a narrow "body" in the form of another tear extending down another seven or eight inches.

How could the hawk escape from this enclosure? Would someone have to rescue it?

I ran to the phone to try to get help. I remember only the call I made to the Laboratory of Ornithology at Cornell University, in Ithaca, New York, a place I had learned about while working at the zoo. The ornithologist I reached thought that the hawk might have been chasing a pigeon that had veered sharply away while very close to my terrace, too late for the hawk to change its direction and causing it to crash through the screen. Or perhaps a captured prey animal had wrenched itself free from the hawk's talons, discombobulating its would-be killer when the hawk was too near the terrace to adjust its flight path.

I had turned away from the terrace to find the laboratory's telephone number on my laptop, and when I looked again, the hawk was gone. It must have found the tear in the screen and flown away to freedom, since the screen was fully intact everywhere else. How did it know to do that? I wish I had seen its progress and regret very much that I hadn't.

In retrospect, I am amazed not only by the hawk's sagacity but also by the behavior of Annie, one of twin kittens a friend had rescued from outdoors a few years earlier. Annie had left the terrace relatively nonchalantly; she certainly had not raced inside when the hawk suddenly appeared. An image of her in mid-stride remains fixed in my memory, like a freeze-frame from a film. Perhaps, having been born in Manhattan to a stray, which itself may have been the descendant of generations of strays, Annie recognized danger only vaguely, having lost the natural instincts of a true feral cat living in wilderness. I also imagine that the hawk felt far too stunned to recognize Annie as prey. I shudder to think what might have happened otherwise.

I thank my addiction to reading novels to my second close encounter with a raptor. Like countless other addicts of every stripe, I tell myself each morning that I will not give in to my addiction that day, at least until I accomplish a certain number of tasks, but I invariably fail. At some point several times daily, I reach for a book, drawn to it as if by a powerful force that I cannot withstand. Lately I've been sitting in bed to read, with pillows resting against the headboard for support. In the mid-morning recently, I looked up from my book and saw my male cat, Andy, lying on the wide sill that I had installed below the window soon after I moved in to my 15th-floor apartment. The sill rests atop a radiator, offering a nice warm spot for Andy to rest on while taking catnaps or looking out the window at the busy streets below.

Andy seemed to be unusually attentive to something, his eyes focused on the top of the part of the air conditioner that juts out of the window adjoining the window he was lying beside. That something proved to be a bird about the height of a pigeon, but it definitely was not a pigeon. I could see only its head from where I was sitting in bed, a head broader and squarer than a pigeon's. The bird seemed to be totally still. Afraid of scaring it off, I very slowly got off the bed and crept slowly and silently over to the window. The bird remained unmoving. It looked to me like a miniature hawk, the top part of its beak, which overhung the bottom slightly, equipped with a sharp, downward-pointing dark tip. Lying at its sharply clawed feet were the remains of another bird—a head with gaping eye sockets, unrecognizable lumps of tissue, scattered feathers, and a severed pink leg. At first I thought it might have been a baby or fledgling, but it seemed early in the year for hatchlings to have arrived, and one of the feathers looked to be about two inches long—too long for a very young bird, I imagined. But I didn't know enough about birds to identify it.

I gaped at the raptor for at least five minutes, and all the while it remained motionless, so I returned to my bed and continued to watch it from there. Andy now stood on his hind legs, his front paws resting atop the indoor part of the air conditioner, his nose not more than an inch from the windowpane. The bird undoubtedly noticed him but remained completely unfazed. Then the bird's head ducked out of sight, and bits of the corpse at its feet began flying rapidly upward in every direction. The wind carry several feathers away.

Suddenly Annie materialized and jumped onto the sill, obviously eager to see what was going on, but Andy—who is at least three times her size—evidently wanted to keep the spectacle all to himself and subtly shooed her off. He himself left the scene shortly afterward, as did the bird, though I'm sorry to say I didn't see it fly away. Perhaps it had had its fill while I was watching the brief interaction between Andy and

Annie. Almost nothing remained on the air conditioner as evidence of what had occurred there.

The diminutive raptor, I discovered on Google within a minute and corroborated by means of Google Images, was almost certainly a common kestrel. (It looked far plainer than the American kestrel, though I may be mistaken.) Also known as the European kestrel or Old World kestrel, the common kestrel is a member of the falcon family. According to Wikipedia, "It is widespread in Europe, Asia, and Africa, as well as occasionally reaching the east coast of North America." If it is really only an occasional visitor, I feel exceedingly fortunate indeed that the bird who came to dinner—who came *with* its dinner—chose my air conditioner as its table.

WRAP-AROUND GIRL

Thais Sherell

She was hurt and in need

I never stopped to think if I should

After all, it might have seemed inappropriate

She in all her years of glory and wisdom, 80 or more

I, full of wisdom too, however paling to hers

It happened instantaneously

I didn't think

Like a child I moved, though in my wisdom I responded

Climbing behind her as she sat, edge-side of her bed

I followed my heart, beaming with love for another's mother

I wrapped my long slender legs around her thickened waist

Using every ounce of love that I could muster from our Father,

I embraced her with my arms

My head gently rested on the back of her neck

There were no words, just love transmitting from my heart to
hers

She was in pain, tears rolled down her cheeks

She moaned, tones that only our Father completely understood

I, in my near forty years of life, understood little

I knew there was pain, deep pain, in this woman so much like
my own

So there I was, half her years and holding her, loving her

through intercession

I would be His arms and legs, time was of the essence

That day would pass and Father saw her through

He saw her through not only one more day but ten or more

years

Years filled with love, laughter, and sometimes pain

I never thought again of that one afternoon except to smile as

her daughter deemed me to be "Mother's Wrap-around Girl"

Was it appropriate? My years said I was grown

Grown folk have limits, don't they?

Maybe, Maybe not

In that moment I wasn't an adult or infant

I was simply God's vessel, ready for duty

DIRTY BIRD

Vilma Luz Cabán

The LP record spun round and round. Disco music was blaring on the record player with a few skips from scratches on the record. "So I'd like to know where, you've got the notion. Don't rock the boat, don't rock the boat baby." The music was playing from inside our neighbor Tony's house, which was down the hall on the 4th floor of our apartment building. Tony was my stepfather's drinking buddy from la bodega and his wife was a quiet lady that didn't have much to say every time my mother greeted her in the elevator. I remember the long walk down the building hall to their apartment. That day my next-door neighbor Tony and his wife were going to babysit my little brother and I, as my mother ran to a doctor's appointment with my baby brother Freddy.

As we approached the door, the music sounded louder, and my mother had to knock hard so that they could hear her knocks. Tony opened the door, and my mother asked for his wife. He told her that she went to the supermarket to get the snacks for the kids to eat. She looked at us and then told Rafy and I to go inside. I obediently did what I was told. My mother thanked him and he closed the door. It felt odd to be alone with him. This was the first time I saw the inside of that apartment. He wasn't a complete stranger to us. I guess my mother trusted him to take care of us because on other occasions, Tony would visit us. Tony was tall, dark, and skinny. He looked more like a Puerto Rican version of Felix Unger from the *Odd Couple* show on television. He smoked Marlboro cigarettes and he chewed violet gum just like my uncle Tio Juan from my Papí's side of the family. He wore bellbottom dress slacks that were very fitted on his hips and waist, along with button down dress shirts with large collars.

In the sunny living room, I spotted a white birdcage by the window. There was a light blue parakeet frantically flying around in his cage with his wings flapping against the metal sides of the cage. I detested his ear-piercing screeches. For such a beautiful bird, he looked miserable on this hot summer day. Their apartment seemed huge compared to our small one-bedroom apartment. They had nicer furniture than us. They had a beautiful record player that looked more like a dresser because it was so long with speakers built in on the sides. The place was very neat, and I figured it was because they didn't have any kids running around all the time. The couple did not have any children and from the vibe that I felt from Tony's wife; I didn't think she liked kids. In the corner of the living room, I spied a pair of shiny black heels by the sofa. Tony encouraged me to take off my sneakers and to put the heels on. They were huge on my feet and when I tried walking in them, my skinny knees would buckle and bump into each other as I tried to straighten myself up and walk properly on them. My little brother Rafy giggled at the sight of his big sister trying to be all grown up tripping with these pointy shoes.

When I turned around, I didn't see Tony and he walked away reappearing with a ball from the bedroom. What else was inside that room? I was curious. I tried peering around his shoulder and saw a small television on a TV cart with wheels. Rafy asked him if we could watch cartoons. Tony spoke English and I was learning a lot of English in school. He turned the dial on the television set and stopped it on to channel 13. Sesame Street was on. My brother immediately planted himself right in front of the television sitting with his legs crossed happy as a clam. He was not interested in the red ball. He wanted to see Big Bird. I thought Sesame Street was for babies.

I wasn't a baby, so I walked back into the living room to check out the bird in the cage. I was going to be an explorer now that the quiet lady was not there to give me strange penetrating looks. Anyway, when was she coming back? As I observed the parakeet flapping his wings and listening to the music in the living room, from the side of my eye I sensed Tony getting closer. He had the red ball in front of him. As he got closer, he asked with a nice voice. "Do you want to play with something?" He threw the red ball onto the sofa and when I turned my head to look at him, he wiggled out from the zipper of his pants. Tony was holding his penis in his hands. I recognized a penis from having to change my little brothers' diapers, but this one looked very different. It was big, dark, wrinkly, and ugly as he rubbed it with his hand. I got scared when I looked at him as he smiled a creepy smile.

I felt cornered standing between the birdcage, the side of the sofa, the wall, and Tony in front of me. Now I knew why that bird screeched. It was trapped just like me. I quickly slipped out of the heels and I told him to stop. I didn't want to play. I felt like I was on some weird loop like the LP record that kept playing over and over again. It was driving me crazy. I wanted it to stop. He got closer and grabbed my hand. He forced me to touch it. His rough hands crushed my thin little fingers around his penis. He wanted me to rub it the way he rubbed it. Then with his other dirty hand he stroked my hair, which was in a side ponytail. He started to pull on my hair and it hurt as my head started to get pulled down closer to his ugly penis. I was so disgusted. I felt like I was going to throw up. When suddenly there was this white stuff that erupted out of a hole in his penis. He grabbed most of it with his hands and brought it closer to my face. Oh my God! He wanted me to smell it or taste this? I desperately refused and shook my head. I said. "I'm telling!"

Tony's ugly face got close to mine and I could smell his cigarette breath. He menacingly said. "If you tell, I will kill your bird Cupo. They won't believe you. You are a bad and dirty little girl. Look at you." I became enraged! With all my might, I punched him in the stomach and squeezed my skinny little body by the side of him. I ran straight into the bedroom to sit with my little brother. I wanted to protect my little brother. My heart was racing. Why did Tony do what he did? I didn't want him to kill my bird. It was strange. It felt dirty and wrong. What was I going to do?

Obliviously happy and content watching television, my brother Rafy looked up at me as I quickly sat down by his side. His little innocent head leaned on my shoulder. He had not heard me say stop. He did not hear our conversation in the living room. He had not heard me run. My heart was racing. I had the oddest sensation that I could see myself from the corner of the room. It was as if I was watching the movie of what was happening to me. I had the strangest taste in my mouth. It was a metallic taste. Did he put some of that disgusting stuff in my mouth? I was so anxious and I remember breathing really hard after running in and sitting by my little brother's side. At that moment, every cell in my body wanted to run out of that place. But I couldn't. I was trapped. Would he come in and make my little brother do the same thing. If he did, I would bite his penis off! What was I going to do? I knew Mami was not home. Where would I go? I couldn't just run out and leave my little brother behind. I prayed that Mami would get back quickly but it felt like she had just left.

I was shaking so much as I sat by my little innocent brother. I was petrified. In that moment, I felt the weirdest sensation. I peed in my pants. There was a yellow puddle on the floor in between my legs. It was a warm sensation that felt more like a release. I smelled the urine as it sat in a puddle below me. I stared at the dark blue stain on my dungaree wide leg pants. Suddenly my brother Rafy said, "Yuck, you peed on yourself". I immediately stood up humiliated and simply stood there frozen like a statue. Tony came into the room, looked down at the yellow pee on the floor and yelled "¡Estupida!" Now my brother could witness that he really was not a nice guy. Tony walked over to me and grabbed me by my skinny right arm so hard that I felt like he was going to pull it right out of my shoulder socket. My little brother looked at him confused and he started to cry pulling me away from Tony's rough grip. Then Tony sighed, released my arm, and quickly stepped out of the room. When he reappeared, Tony walked into the room with a mop in his hand. The music was still blaring. Then I got an idea. I firmly held my brothers' hand, and slowly placed a finger on my lip to signal him to stay quiet. Then little by little I led Rafy out of the room watching closely as Tony mopped the floor from side to side. He was not looking at me and that is when I made a dash with my little brother to the door! My best friend and neighbor Lisa lived upstairs. Her apartment was on the fifth floor right by the staircase. It was no less than 10 feet from the apartment door. We both ran down the dark hallway to the front door. I quickly unlocked the door. Then I picked up Rafy as I made a quick dash for the steps by the apartment door. After racing up the landing, I frantically knocked on Lisa's door. I could still hear the music downstairs spilling out into the echoing chamber of the hallway. "So I'd like to know where you got the notion. Said I'd like to know where you got the notion."

THE DAY THE WAR ENDED

Suzan Rotgard

I was home with Grandma, which was not at all unusual. She frequently took care of me while my mother was at work or wherever else she may have been. Sometimes Grandma picked me up from nursery school and even stayed with me overnight.

I had been playing in my room alone. My bed was on the wall next to the door to my room. A small dresser and a bookcase with books and toys on its shelves took up the opposite wall. There was only one other room in the apartment with a tiny kitchenette at one end of it. My mother slept there and my Grandma, too, when she stayed over. We had our own bathroom inside of our apartment.

Suddenly, there was lots of noise coming from the street, which all of our windows farced. I was frightened and confused. I had never heard such a commotion before. What could it be? Grandma said something about the war, and I thought she meant that the war was here. By then, she was looking out the window and I joined her. Outside people filled the street and the sidewalks. Some paged instruments. Some were banging on the tops of garbage cans. They were all yelling and singing and dancing—yes, dancing—in the street. "Is that the war? Is the war here?" I asked Grandma. Could that explain the unusual chaos down below? "No," she replied. "It is not. Today the war is over." People were very happy. They danced and sang and made lots of noise for hours and hours. And Grandma and I watched from our window for hours and hours.

Grandma and I looked out the window often. It was fun, and I really liked it. I guess she did too. In those days there weren't many cars on the streets. There were, however, always lots of people. One person who walked up and down our street, who maybe even lives on our street, had two big, beautiful dogs that were always with her. (Now that I think of it, in those days there weren't that many dogs on the street, either.) Many years later, I found out that they were called the pantaloon dogs. We looked for them every day.

A while later, Grandma decided that it was time for me to have my supper. I wasn't particularly hungry, and I was content to keep watching the fascinating activity below. Grandma was convinced that I didn't eat enough, that I was undernourished and would fall ill and who knows what would happen. She believed that basically from the time I was born.

Soon it was time for me to get washed up and go to bed. I fell asleep thinking that the war is over and feeling happy about it. The noise in the street continued way into the night, long after I fell asleep.

THE AFTERMATH

B. Lynn Carter

In abject blackness, I drifted through the aftermath. The flames had been extinguished. There were shadows, ghostly impressions of familiar items, barely recognizable. Gone was the fragile mirrored music box that once played "Ain't Misbehaving." Missing was that resounding sound, that steady . . . tick . . . tick . . . tick . . . of Papa's wind-up clock that never, ever went un-wound. Absent, the metal-clad telephone, black and heavy. The weighty oversized receiver that used to dwarf my face . . . gone.

The fragrance of loose powder and Taboo had been replaced by the acrid smell of melted plastic, the stench of burnt wood and paper. The flames . . . the actual flames, had completely spared Momma's downstairs living quarters but the intense heat . . . and the intense firemen had not. They came with sirens howling through the streets of the Bronx, they came to save us. They came. They were an avenging tsunami. They brought a wall of water, a deluge. Then, they proceeded to smash and destroy all that had actually survived the flames.

Or so it seemed to me at the time.

On that mid-winter's night, it was as black as despair and as cold as a crypt. Everything was encased in ice. Everyone was infused with ice. Ice crackled under feet with every step. Something inside me stirred, stretched, expanded in my lungs. My breath wheezed in my chest.

I splintered.

Thankfully, a 'me' outside of me emerged. She took my hand and guided me through the ruins. Yes, my mind did space away that night, just briefly, as I contemplated the relationship between fire and ice, saviors and . . . interior desecrators.

Or so it seemed.

The glare of flashlights snatched me back, shook me into the moment. Crisscrossing beams cut through the black void, casting sinister shadows as my grief-stricken family picked through the remains, seeking the salvageable.

Gory plastic stalactites, like tentacles frozen and glazed, dribbled downward. Witches claws, they threatened to grab that "me" outside of me, as I dazed past.

A beam flashed. In a sooty blue glass mirror, my reflection flickered, split, straddled a rickety fissure, my face fractured, cracked and disjointed. So, on that wretched night this question eased across my mind. Mirror, mirror, who's been shattered most of all?

MY TEN AND HALF YEAR OLD PERSPECTIVE

Lady Tiffany

My heart is overwhelmed at the rough age of 10 and a half. I am reaching for truth in a territory of lies. Feeling lost trying to understand all these adult problems that seem so foolish to me but what do I know?

He arrived at the door with another woman, came inside and went into my momma's bathroom. My mom was at school. My brother, and I were waiting anxiously for her to come home. She always came ready with a big hug and bearing snacks of course. I had done all my chores and properly washed my brother up. We had lasagna for lunch and dinner, courtesy of momma's ready-made Tupperware meals prepared for the whole week.

The doorbell rings and I get excited, thinking "my mother must have so many goodies she can't use her keys!" I open the door and he's standing there with his raspy voice, and I hear a woman's voice that is not my mother's.

"My mother's not here yet." I say.

"I'm here to wait for her." he says as he brushes past me, with the women following him into the bathroom.

I lost it. I've already seen my mother go off on my father and stepfather for indiscretions that where blatantly disrespectful. I get my brother dressed in a fury to wait for mommy downstairs.

"Mommy will get to the bottom of this and make them go away and never return." I thought to myself.

I was frightened and didn't understand why my mom even liked him, he seemed icky, but he made her laugh, and she wasn't lonely anymore. So, I just went with it and she seemed happy.

But I was sure that this move would get him booted out of our lives for sure. All I had to do was wait for her return, in the meantime I watch my little brother play and keep an eye on him. I felt proud and responsible. A big girl who was worthy of a hug and an extra treat.

Then finally I saw her face and ran over to her yelling "mommy!" She kissed me and asked why I was outside, her expression panicked and face flushed. I started to ramble off the details of this incident that provoked my movements to come outside after dark. Surely she would see things my way, and how I was justified to do such drastic action.

We got my little brother and go into the building. She starts breathing heavy, and looked angry but the anger felt extremely justified

"I got your back mommy; we will handle this!" I think to myself. Preparing for whatever may happen when she opens the door. Praying to God that he won't be violent like my stepfather was when she confronted him.

She tells me to go to my room and take my baby brother. I am hesitant because I want him to know that I am aware of his deplorable actions and that my mother would not allow her kids or home to be disrespected in that manner!

I go to my room, and I hear some loud voices and then nothing but the TV. I go out to talk to my mother and make sure she is ok. But as I peek into the living room, I see his shoes that are not on his feet, and he's just sitting there on my sofa, drunk and seemingly unbothered. I'm perplexed by his calm demeanor. My mother suddenly seemed okay with this incident. I couldn't help but ask he why he's still here? She tells me to go to my room. I am filled with anxiety and disappointment, and I don't feel safe with him in the house. I begin to cry and he tells me to hush.

"No! get out!" I yell with tears flowing down my cheeks.

My mommy grabs my arm and takes me to the bathroom. With this look of disappointment and anger on her face.

I start bawling uncontrollably "Why is he still here? Why mommy? Why is he still here? He brought another woman in our house and just came in without even asking if I was comfortable."

I cry and scream but she starts to yell at me, focusing on the fact I took my brother out the house after dark and for being disrespectful to an adult. She pops me on my lips; my heart sinks deep in my stomach from betrayal and defeat. How could I be wrong for wanting to protect her virtue and sanctity of our home, wasn't that the reason you made my father leave? Aren't my feelings and emotional safety valid enough to at least explain to me why you let this drunk man, whom I for some reason feel threatened by, stay in our home that is supposed to be my sanctuary. My safe place has now become a hostile environment.

My life changed drastically as did the way I saw my mother. The level of respect I had for her slowly diminished through the years of disrespect and tears that left me numb as I succumbed to the environment set before me. A road and path that got me kicked out of my home at 14 years old.

All this to say who knows the messages we send to our children minds how we may disregard their spirit and intellect, all for the human need to be loved but at what cost?

BLOSSOMING IN THE BRONX:
A CHILD'S STORY

Don Carlos Ramirez

My mother Anna Isabel was a slim beautiful vibrant 5'3 tan skin Puerto Rican with almond shaped eyes and shiny long black hair; she was also a gifted singer and well educated young bride. Father was taller, muscular and although a handsome carpenter, he looks old and tired most of the time. I am the youngest of 3 siblings and also the only female; I am Celia Estelle 10 years old and mother's twin, fat Jaime, "Gordo" is 11 and Leonel "mop stick," because he is tall and athletic looking like dad, is 13.

The only advantage to being the only girl is that I am the last to get to soak in a bath all by myself even though by then the water temperature has cooled down enough to chill my skin;
but the boys can only enjoy a quick standing up only shower and have no private time to daydream. But they don't complain because boys like being sweaty, smelly and dirty.

In my encyclopedia books I see many different countries to visit with so many events to sign up for. And once you get there, a lot of beautiful stores to walk into and browse or do some real shopping. But I am not old enough to make it on my own yet so I must depend on my parents for when they believe what leisure activity I can participate in, the proper entertainment for me to see and be a part of, and even who I can or cannot socialize with; and also the right time. God how I wish I was 18 already. Every day at home, my family life is in turmoil; everyone is constantly barking so many unfair orders and commands and arguing that I sometimes wish I could totally disappear away from them. Still, on some occasions I manage to retaliate a little against my brother's constant trying to control or push me around by causing them to get the blame for some mischief I purposely created to make it look like they had a hand in the process. But when it comes to my mother and father assigning me chores and how to conduct myself ladylike or sternly reminding me who is in charge, it takes a lot more finessing at exploiting their soft "emotional" areas to get around their absolute authority and power, especially when I am facing a possible spanking. Life in a family of 5 has its good moments as well as many harsh ones I guess. And it's not that much different at school either for it seems that their rules are the same; I must sit quietly inside a small crowded room being obligated by one controlling dictatorial person to learn math, science, read, write and speak English or else there's some form of punishment to expect.

English is such a complicated language that is almost entirely foreign to me, since I have only been living in New York for two years and its only use is for whenever I am outdoors and must socialize. I must also learn to navigate around the many other ethnic groups of boys and girls whose sole job is to poke fun at my thick Spanish accent and make fun when I wear my brother's hand-me-down clothing.

On the other hand, the children of recently transplanted parents are nice and we are civil toward each other, but most of the children who bully us act out according to whatever behaviors they have learnt from their parents, family, seen from televised distorted programs or have been ridiculed by other older bullies. I guess not being able to fully stand up for myself in English does have its disadvantages; unless there are more of your kind present, than of those of them doing the disparaging—get it! Then I only have to contend with their looks of disdain and possibly getting picked on or beaten up once I separate from "the pack." Whenever I tell my parents of all the harassments I must deal with, they remind me that I must simply obey the rules, be fair and learn how to mingle with my peers. My teacher calls this abuse learning to socialize, coping, joining forces, and taking one for the team in order to build confidence. I call it a whole lot of something else, but I am not allowed to repeat that.

My parents make all of the decisions for me and father has decided that I'm growing so up fast, that I have become a bit stubborn and just as sensitive like mother. Mother says that this will soon pass as I adjust to my adolescence and the reason I now cry easily and feel kind of trapped is because I recently got my period and my body and mind are a bit confused. Yeah right, I think that father is nothing but a big bully himself and that mother is the one who is confused.

This new neighborhood has a lot of boys who think that they are grown up men and I don't feel very safe around these teenagers who cut class and now hang out in front of the stoop of our building smoking, drinking wine and disrespecting us girls when we arrive after we are let out from school. Some of the girls smile way too much at them too, and I believe that this habit only encourages those boys to one day try something naughty or stupid with us that they ain't supposed to. Mother once said that, that is how many girls won't ever get to finish school and how some boys get into trouble when they want to act like grown men. Mama tried to teach me how I should wear a tight cloth over my breasts so that my chest looks flat and I look younger but that is not helping me any longer because my breasts seem to have a mind of their own and they want to be out there and be seen; I'm so stressed out. But on the other hand, there's this fine looking boy named Tony and although he hangs out too, I am attracted and fascinated with his hazel eyes, shiny wavy long black hair and a rock solid six pack rack. Tony is tall and slim like dad too. I won't smile at Tony when I enter my building; he's just too old and way too cool for my own good. Still, I sometimes can't help myself and as I walk up the stairs, the grown-up girl inside me wants his company, sighs deeply and I let out a light giggle. I'm afraid one day he's going to hear me, follow behind and stop me; and then he'll do something naughty. Oh, just thinking about him makes me tingle just about everywhere, all over my body. I guess those wicked thoughts are worth an ear pull if mother ever caught me lingering on my staircase, and also earn me 'bout nine "Our

Father's" and ten "Hail Mary's" this coming Saturday afternoon after I finish my church sins confessional.

My father is a 6 foot 11 inch tall muscular stern unsmiling man, with long thick large fingers.

Everyone avoids having any contact or dealings with him. And ever since the boys learned that he is my dad; they won't dare make any loud-mouthed comments whenever I enter my building alone. In fact, when father arrives early from working at the funeral parlor after reconstructing caskets, the boys step aside; like Moses just parted the sea; or like he had some black magic demonic smoke coming out from him. That's also the signal for them to quietly and immediately take off. "I hate you daddy for scaring off Tony away from my chance to one day sigh loudly as I pass him by hoping he'll follow." Even with all the stress of soon coming into the new world of a teenager, it is great growing up in my Bronx; because soon there will be a vacation break to look forward to and I'll be spending time at Orchard beach with its warm shore waters draping my body where in my mind I shall secretly spend a quiet afternoon of passion and receiving an embrace from Tony's strong arms. "Despierta de esos sueños Celia Estelle; wake up dreamy girl it's time for school. Oh, for heaven's sake mom."

JUST ONE MORE THING

Barbara Lyne

It wasn't raining, so that couldn't account for the dreariness I felt that day walking up to North Bronx Central Hospital. It wasn't even cloudy. But my sister had had another convulsion and today she was to come home from the hospital.

Walking up the Grand Concourse I had a visual recollection of the day I walked into our apartment and it was quiet which was unusual. No TV and my mother sitting on the living room couch with a gentle look of quiet concern.

"I don't know where Alice is," she spoke softly. "I don't remember her going out, but I don't know where she is." Our mother, housebound, marooned, couldn't get up to look and see. I could just imagine my mother's concern, having sat there softly calling Alice's name and wondering why there was no reply when she was sure she hadn't left.

I went into her bedroom to see if she was simply taking a nap and found her conscious but convulsed on the floor. By now I had become used to what that meant: she needed a change in her prescribed medications. It probably should've been done a few days ago, but it had to be done in a supervised setting and you couldn't admit someone to the hospital because of an impending condition. So that meant you'd have to either rob a bank so you'd have money for private rehab, or go down to Fordham Road and create a commotion so bad that when the police came they'd take you away and have you committed. Or, the third and usual option was to go into convulsion, call 911 and be told by a 'competent authority' that your meds needed changing.

So, as I crossed Mosholu Parkway it seemed to me a simple thing of picking her up with her new prescription, getting something for lunch for the three of us and getting a cab home. So then, how was I to understand this mild feeling of dreariness turning slowly to dread.

When I entered her hospital room, Alice was in the bathroom just washing up. As she turned to me, I noticed she didn't look any better, whatever that even was anymore. She said only three words as she led me to the bed to sit down.

"I have news."

Brevity of expression is something I can appreciate, but I needed more. When we were seated she said another three words,

"I have cancer."

We hugged, we cried a little and then I gave her my best imitation of a deer caught in headlights. She said, gently, "Barbara, I only hope that you can think of this the way I think of it."

I just couldn't imagine.

"How do you think of it?" I asked through shallow breath. To which she simply replied, "Barbara, it's just one more thing."

What a life lesson! The dreariness slowly dissolved as I came to realize, my big sister is the best.

THE BRONX STANDS FOR MUSIC

Sonia Fuentes-Resto

I have always defined myself by the music of my being, my essence. Whether it's in the vinyl record collection, cassette tapes, IPOD or my phone, there's a song for the various times of my life. My trajectory of music started long ago right here in the Bronx.

We had just finished moving into our new five room apartment on the first floor. The cluster of various sized boxes, stuffed pillowcases, paper shopping bags ready to burst held all of our belongings. My grandmother closely guarded her worn trunk filled with her life-long possessions. My parents used every ragged suitcase they could borrow to carry their past dreams and disillusions. I remember that all of my worldly goods fit into one bureau drawer. This was 1959 and my folks did not have the luxury of hiring movers or for buying large boxes for packing. In fact, they probably got the boxes from the old bodega or whatever neighborhood store was getting rid of them.

The first thing I noticed about our new building at 1047 Home Street, in the South Bronx, was the enormous tiled entrance hallway and the adjacent vestibule. Our old building was tiny. It didn't seem important at the time, but just as I stepped out and called for someone, I heard an echo of my voice. It resonated, lingered for a moment and then it stopped as abruptly as it started. As an eight-year-old I quickly learned how to use it just for fun. What I didn't know was that this was the playroom for teenagers that sang. One afternoon as I was doing homework, I heard the enchanting voices of homemade Doo Wop right there in my hallway. My brother, Junior was singing with two African American teens and one Italian singing lead. They were singing "In the Still of the Night" by the Five Saints. My ears and soul although youthful, immediately recognized the magic sounds being created. We were all searching for the music that defined us or that moved us.

My older brothers listened to the Doo Wop station on the one radio we had in the living room as soon as they arrived from school. The top 40's were played on various stations but they preferred WINS 1010 with Murray the K. Doo Wop music was created by African American youth back in the 1940's. It was a popular urban sound in the northeast especially New York, Pittsburg and Philadelphia. Groups consisted of trios or quartets backing up the lead singer. Their voices had to be in different vocal ranges such as the bass singer keeping the melody and rhythm and the tenor with highest voice as the lead. The group provided backing harmonies all singing a cappella with no instrumentation. This made sense to city teenagers of all backgrounds who couldn't afford music classes or instruments. The lyrics were usually messages depicting lost love, unrequited love, new love, far away or secret love. All topics we can relate to in our youth. At the time, I certainly did not understand the secret messages. I struggled to understand what the words meant. I repeated the "Ten Commandments of Love" by the Moonglows as I heard them. Little did I know that the verses stood for rules of fidelity, blind faith, "take happiness with the heartaches" or "kiss me when you hold me tight." My seventy-year-old grandmother asked my brothers what I was singing. When they told her, she stood up and escorted me by my arm away from the radio. All I knew was that this music was being heard by all teenagers in the family, in the neighborhood and on American bandstand on television. I didn't understand what was out of line about the lyrics then but I learned to listen prudently as I grew older. The words described the angst of all young people who think they're falling in love. We all want to hear that others share our pain or confusion.

Of course, the Bronx was home to its own famous Doo Wop groups like Dion and the Belmonts, Larry Chance and the Earls and female group, The Shantells. Some members of these groups are alive today and still perform because Doo Wop has remained a favorite genre for many. In the late fifties, all Bronx teenagers Puerto Rican, African American, Italian and Irish listened to this unique music that could be replicated in hallways, high school bathrooms and when the group polished its songs, they would perform on street corners. That was magical. Parents with reservations about their teens listening or performing Doo Wop were suddenly proud to listen to the creative sounds emanating from the neighborhood kids. This was something that would repeat itself later on.

By 1960, my brothers, Junior and Harry started to listen to another type of music. It was known all over the world as Latin music. This music emanated from Cuba and our ancestral roots from Spain and Africa. I became fascinated by the change in the teens in our family. All of a sudden, they started speaking and singing in Spanish. That motivated me to re-learn Spanish also. School and outside cultural pressures had forced us to forget our native language. This was an exciting new world of two cultures and a bridge connecting us to our parent's origins. It was through music that we grew and accepted others. Music never stopped playing in my childhood home. My parents had purchased a console radio and stereo for the entire family. They played 78rpm records for their house parties while my brothers purchased precious long-playing albums of the top Latin bands in New York City such as Machito, Tito Puente and Tito Rodríguez. They went to watch them live at the famous Palladium nightclub on 53rd Street. It was the mecca for dancing mambo and it attracted people of all races, religions and regardless of economic status, which was highly unusual for pre-civil rights America. It lasted from the late 1940's to the early 1960's. Once it closed, Latin music patrons looked for other large dance halls and they found them in the Bronx.

The neighborhood youth knew that we had a stereo and that my brothers had the latest recordings of the great Latin stars and Harry was now playing timbales along with the music. Young men and women would come by to listen and play an instrument or dance. I would ogle the nineteen or twenty-year-old ladies who came over in their stylish capri pants and Audrey Hepburn flat shoes to practice dance moves in my living room. Their partner-dancing had to be perfect, in rhythm and in time. Once the male took the lead and lifted her arm to turn, the female had to measure her steps internally and turn gracefully, in step, to be ready for the next move. Oh, I wanted to dance exactly like her when I grew up. I yearned to wear that red lipstick and brilliantine oil in my hair. On club nights these ladies came to our apartment to show off their tight mermaid shaped dresses and leave a trace of Evening in Paris perfume.

Latin music has remained in my life like an old friend, always there for the right occasions. I became one of those twenty-year-olds in my childhood living room. Dancing, practicing and primping for those determinate night of club dancing. I can listen to a thirty-year-old song and remember exactly what I wore and who I tried to impress with my dancing. I listen to Latin music when I'm walking, cooking or writing. Notice that I don't call it Salsa. That is a commercial title and not the original classification. Latin music gives me energy, warmth and definition. It is who I am. I'm so proud that famous musicians like Eddie Palmieri lived in the same Bronx neighborhood where I was born, Kelly Street. Others like Tito Puente, Johnny Pacheco and Joe Quijano all went to school or played music on that same street. That area had some of the most famous Latin night clubs in the 1950's and 1960's, The Bronx Music Palace, El Tropicoro, El Tropicana, The Carousel and The Tritons, a famous after-hours club that many senior Bronxites remember. It was the gathering place for all famous bandleaders and musicians for special live recordings and the birthplace of the "Pachanga" dance. The Bronx continues to host Latin music dances at various clubs and concerts at Lehman College and Hostos College. The borough has the distinction of being named "El Condado de La Salsa" by radio DJ's for many years.

As my family grew so did the music being heard at gatherings and Sunday dinners during the 1970's. My brother's children listened to Hip Hop; a sub-genre of music born in the Bronx. My initial reaction was to recoil at the repetitive lyrics and rhythm but then I got it. I understood the youth's search for identity and expression. This music essentially started in parties on Sedgewick Avenue with the use of an amplifier and two turntables. Next was the incorporation of isolating sounds and reusing them, known as "sampling," "breakbeat," which was playing the same song on the two turntables and "scratching," a sound we all recognize in music today. "Rapper's Delight" by the Sugar Hill Gang or "Planet Rock" by Soulsonic Force became worldwide hits. My nephews became DJ's of this new sound and were successful at family parties. We were proud.

Another music phenomenon partially born in the Bronx, in the 1980's was "Freestyle," for Hispanic and Italian American youth looking to create a fusion of Latin music, vocal disco styles with electronic instrumentation and syncopated percussion. This was yet another example of young people yearning to express their identity and emotions through music. My brother Harry, my parents, frowned on the repetitive nature of the music as I also did. We tried to listen and probably best understood the lyrics, again about lost love or new love. Nayobe's "Please Don't Go" or Lil Suzy's "Take Me in Your Arms" had a new sound and dance rhythm for me but the message was clearly the same. A Puerto Rican woman like me, from the Bronx can identify with a love message through Doo Wop, Latin, Hip Hop or Freestyle music. That is why the Bronx represents music for many who have lived or visited here. Our diversity is expressed, mixed and widely accepted through our music. Besides, it is the true story of my life.

BETWEEN THE LINES: MESSAGES FROM MY FAMILY IN CUBA

Katarina Wong

Until I was 13, I only knew my mother's side of the family from the letters that appeared in our mailbox in distinctive red and blue striped envelopes. Tight, cursive handwriting declared my mother's full name: Lucia Capin Wong, the only time I ever saw her family name attached to ours. The weeks it took those letters to cross the ninety miles between Cuba and Florida made each envelope feel like a winning lottery ticket.

"Mooooooom!! A letter from Cuba!" my sisters and I would cry as we ran in with the mail.

"*Dámela!* Give it to me!" Mom would stop whatever she was doing to hurry over. She'd carefully slice open an edge of the envelope, smooth out the pages, and read their contents. Sometimes it would be a single letter; sometimes the envelope would contain several letters from different relatives.

"*Querida hermana*...Dear sister..."

"*Querida tía*...Dear aunt..."

"*Querida hija*...Dear daughter..."

"*Querida prima*...Dear cousin..."

Precious stories about their lives would unfold from those onion skin thin sheets. Who got married, who was pregnant, who went to Havana, how the tobacco crops were. Sometimes part of a letter would be mysteriously redacted in heavy black marker. My family were mostly poor, rural people. *What state secrets could they possibly know?* I wondered.

I never saw my mother writing back, although I knew she always did. I imagine her sitting at our dining table late at night when the house was finally quiet, the kitchen cleaned, my sisters and I tucked in bed, and dad watching TV in another room. Maybe then, exhausted from cleaning houses during the day and working as a caterer at night, she would finally have a few moments to pull out similar thin sheets of paper and tell her family about her life in America.

*"Querida hermana...*Dear sister..."

*"Querido hermano...*Dear brother..."

*"Querido papá...*Dear father..."

*"Querida prima...*Dear cousin..."

Sometimes, the envelopes from Cuba showed up a bit fatter than usual, and that was cause for extra excitement.

"Mooooooooom!! A letter from Cuba! I think it's got photos!"

My sisters and I would gather tightly around her as she pulled a chair to the kitchen table.

We were eager for the show-and-tell about to come.

"Who's that? Is that *tía* Raquel? Is that grandpa?" we'd demand.

"Esperan, niñas! Let me read the letter first!"

She'd translate the letter to us then carefully spread the images across the floral tablecloth. We would lean in to examine those black and white peeks into our family's lives.

Mom would point out who was who, etching their faces in our minds and in hers.

Sparked by the photographs, she would tell us about her life in Cuba. "I remember," her stories would begin. "I was walking home at night. I was very young—maybe five?—and I had to pass by the *guardia,* where the soldiers kept their horses. I was so scared of them, especially the big, black stallion. He looked like he wanted to trample me. I would always run past as fast as I could! This photo of your cousin Mayra is taken right next door to where those horses were kept."

I'd heard versions of her stories before, but it didn't matter. Like a favorite fairy tale, I never tired of them and each photo added details to the sketches I had drawn in my mind of our family. On those special afternoons letters, photos, memories all intertwined to become an invisible, unbreakable thread that mended the space between Florida and Cuba and, if only temporarily, the hole in my mother's heart.

My sisters and I first went to Cuba in 1979. Our grandfather was dying, and Mom managed to get special permission to take us to meet him.

My mother came to New York in 1960 as a 26-year old eager to see the world, but then got stuck here when relations between the two countries broke off six months after. On her return to Cuba nearly 20 years later, she found one generation had grown old and another had sprung up. Life had gone on without her, and there was much she needed to catch up on despite the letters we received.

To me, the photos seemed to come alive during that visit. My relatives were both familiar and unfamiliar, like a figment of a vivid dream. That visit, so bittersweet, was the only time I would see my grandfather, but it was also the start of other relationships.

Eventually my *tía* Raquel got a phone line, and Mom would dial and dial and dial until we finally were able to get through. Sometimes it would take hours or even days, but then...

"Lucia!!!" excited voices would crackle through the poor connection, and I imagined my aunt and cousins pressed up against the heavy rotary phone receiver, straining to hear

Mom on the other end. Calls were prohibitively expensive, so my mother only called once or twice a year and spoke especially fast, never allowing herself more than a couple of minutes. Those voices helped sustain her between letters and her next visit many years later.

By the 1990s Mom and I were traveling to Cuba regularly—sometimes once a year, sometimes every three years, depending on who was in the Oval Office—and I began to understand the longing that still inhabited my mother. Those trips reminded me that part of my heart was beating there. The more I returned, the louder I heard its beat.

"Querida sobrina… Dear niece..."

"Querida amiga… Dear friend..."

"Querida prima… Dear cousin..."

In 2014 my relatives began to have email access, and their messages started to pop up in my inbox. In the past, our letters were a one-way reporting of events. Now I'm able to have conversations with them the way I do with everyone else in my life.

I've come to know that my aunt Emma loves the cinema, that she spends her vacation every December at the Latin American film festival in Havana, carefully taking notes on each movie. When she found a lump had grown back in her breast, I was able to communicate with her quickly about her cancer treatment, offer encouragement in the days post-chemo, and get the news of her remission the same day she heard.

My emails with my cousin Omara focus on practical matters. We write about her job in television production and where they're filming next, what her mother Raquel needs ("Could you bring a battery-powered lamp for the blackouts?

Underwear? Canned food?"), and how hard it is to find toilet paper one month, eggs another, the general disappearance of a host of other necessities.

I know Omara loves Nutella and biographies of historic women; that my artist friends Aylén and Liz need paint brushes and their dog Dante was ill; that my friend Valentina is partial to parmesan cheese, the kind in the green cylinder, and is dating someone new. I tell them about my boyfriend, my cat, how the dark the winter days depress me and how happy I am when the first green signs of spring appear. Back and forth, we reveal ourselves to one another through large and small details of our lives.

When I see their names in my inbox, I feel the same surge of excitement I did as a child, and I hurry home after work to call my mother.

"Mom! I heard from Cuba!"

"Really! Who wrote?" I imagine her sitting at her kitchen table still covered in a floral tablecloth, as I sit down at mine in New York City, the evening light softening into night. I put her on speaker and her voice fills the room.

"What do they say?"

"Just a second, just a second! Let me open the email," I'll reply before reading the latest message.

THE END

Made in the USA
Middletown, DE
02 November 2019